Youth Baseball/Softball Drills, Plays. and Situations Handbook

By Bob Swope
1st Edition 2007

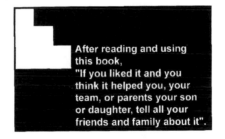

After reading and using this book,
"If you liked it and you think it helped you, your team, or parents your son or daughter, tell all your friends and family about it".

Jacobob **Press** L.L.C.

Published and Distributed By:
Jacobob Press LLC
St. Louis, MO.
(314) 843-4829

ISBN 0-9772817-8-7
SAN 257-1862

Printed and Bound by:
IPC Graphics
Manchester, MO.

First Edition 2007

*******WARNING*******

If your child or the participant has any physically limiting condition, bleeding disorder, high blood pressure, pregnancy or any other condition that may limit them physically you should check with your doctor before letting them participate in any of these, drills or plays.

Be sure participants in these drills and plays that might make hard contact with any of the other participants are all approximately of the same weight and size to avoid a possible injury.

All the drills and plays for kids, should be supervised by an competent adult, coach, or a professional. **AUTHOR ASSUMES NO LIABILITY FOR ANY ACCIDENTAL INJURY OR EVEN DEATH THAT MAY RESULT.**

Extra care and caution should be taken with any of the various batting and outfield catching drills and plays, as they are the more dangerous ones.

Bob Swope
Jacobob Press LLC
Publisher

TABLE OF CONTENTS

Introduction

Intent

Many youth coaches have asked me about easily identified offensive and defensive plays and drills they can use. This book is intended to be a supplemental book to my "Learn'n More About Baseball & Softball" book. It is oriented more towards team coaches on youth teams rather than parents at home teaching fundamentals. We will break this down into what they are doing at the time and what plays to use that will accomplish your goals. My suggestion is, use the time you have each weak to maximize what you want to teach. For little kids it's better to break practice drills down into more than one small group to keep everyone busy.

Training Sessions

Then keep the group training to around 15 minute sessions, blow your whistle, and rotate the kids from one group to the next group. In other words always keep all your kids busy doing something at all times except for water breaks. Don't have any kids just standing around waiting. You get more teaching in this way, the kids don't get bored, and they learn more this way. Get as many assistant coaches as they will let you have, then explain to them what you want each one to teach at their group station. Time wise plan your whole practice session. The kids will then learn more in the short periods of time you have for teaching each week.

The Opponent

It's probably smart to try and understand what the teams you play against are doing against you offensively and defensively. Especially after you have played them once you should have a good idea who their best batters and pitchers are. Keep a small pad of paper in your pocket and take notes. Then what you want to do for a game plan is, pick the offense or defense strategies that will counter, and defeat, what they are doing. Have a game plan before you go into a game, and make sure all your coaches and kids know what it is. Also have a back up plan just in case your main game plan is not working like you expected.

Drills

I am going to refer to the drills as "Skill Training Activities" because that's what they really are. Also I am going to throw in a term now being used a lot. It is called "Core Training". What it does is train their body to make certain moves that will make them a better Baseball/Softball player. Skill activities will be organized by *"numbers"* so that you can have your assistant coaches use them and become more familiar with them that way.

Plays

For easy reference the plays and situations will be organized by *"numbers"* also. They will be arranged as Offensive and Defensive plays. The legend page will show you the symbols for player movement, fly balls, ground balls, and thrown balls. Each play or situation will have a short explanation for how it is supposed to work, strong points, and what it is designed to accomplish.

Strategies

The first strategy I recommend is "have a game plan" to match the team you are playing. Remember though these are only kids, so coach accordingly with your strategies. You know the old "KISS" (Keep-It-Simple-Stupid) phrase. Here are some you can use:

For Offense

1. If you have a team of players that are not too good at hitting, do more bunting at first until they get better. If allowed in your division, teach them how to run the bases and steal.
2. If you have a good hitting team, space out your best hitters so that you have fast speedy runners out on base ahead of them. This is especially important if you have to bat the whole lineup (CYC) instead of just 9 in the batting order.
3. Have signals in place so that your batters and runners on base know exactly what you want them to do in each different situation.

4. In the case of T-Ball leagues, teach your players the different ways to hit the ball. Such as getting underneath the ball to hit it over the heads of the opposing infielders. Or how to aim it between the opposing infielders.

For Defense

1. Place your better youth league fielding players at third base and shortstop where most of the hits go.
2. Make sure your players know early on what the different infield playing depths are. And show them how to shift around a little depending what the batters tendencies might be, to keep ground balls from going through.
3. Make sure your players know early on how to make the different double plays because sometime it takes little kids years of practice to turn one.
4. Teach them to get the lead runner whenever possible when runners are on base, and how to tell when NOT to go for the lead runner.
5. Make sure they know how to back up their bases, and go out to become a cutoff relay infielder on balls hit past or over the head of your outfielders.
6. Make sure they know how to position themselves to tag runners coming into a base.
7. And last make sure they always know how many outs there are, and to think ahead of time by asking themselves what they are going to do if the ball comes to them.

Legend for Diagrams

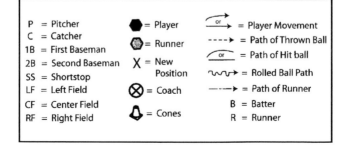

P   = Pitcher
C   = Catcher
1B = First Baseman
2B = Second Baseman
SS = Shortstop
LF = Left Field
CF = Center Field
RF = Right Field

⬡ = Player
◉ = Runner
X = New Position
⊗ = Coach
⏏ = Cones

⟶ or ⟶ = Player Movement
---- ▸ = Path of Thrown Ball
⌒ or ⌒ = Path of Hit ball
∿∿▸ = Rolled Ball Path
—·--▸ = Path of Runner
B = Batter
R = Runner

Offensive Plays

There are a number of offensive plays your players need to know. These are plays they need to know and execute when they are up at bat, or a runner out on the bases.

Simple Basic Offensive Plays

Hitting to the Opposite Field (No.1)

When you are batting right handed (most) you would try to hit the ball to right field. When you are batting left handed you would try to hit the ball to left field. Why teach your team to do this. This is because many teams have their weakest fielder in right field. The ball may have a better chance of getting by them, and you have a good chance of scoring. This is especially true for right handed batters (most) because the defense expects them to pull the ball and hit it to left field.

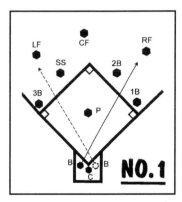

Hitting Behind the Runner (No.2)

This is a play where you want to move a runner up one or two bases, using a play with the best chance of moving them along. As an example if you have runners on first or first and second. Then the batter wants to hit the ball to right field behind them. If the batter hits the ball towards left field, there is a better chance or possibility the defense can tag the runner or throw them out. This is especially true for ground balls hit ahead of a runner.

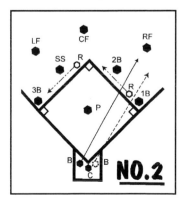

Slap Hitting (NO.3)

Some of your young players are not going to ever be good hitters. Maybe their swing is all wrong or they just can't seem to get it right as they start out. Slap hitting is where you have them wait on the pitch until the last minute, then just slap or flick their bat at the ball. Batters can learn to slap down on the ball for a bouncing ground ball, or slap just under the center to get it just over the infielders heads. Where they will want to aim it will depend on if

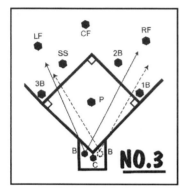

they just want to get on base or move runners along. All it takes is just meeting the ball with a little slap at it move with their bat. If they just need to get a hit with no runners on base, they want to slap ground balls between third base and shortstop. Or just slap it over the heads of the second baseman and first baseman. This will give them the best chance to get on base.

Sacrifices (NO.4,5)

Some of time you may just want to advance a runner on base. Maybe it's a tight low scoring game and you need a run, or runs, badly. Then have your batter *"sacrifice bunt" (NO.4)*. With a runner on first and no one on second, have them bunt towards first. With a runner on second, have them bunt towards third. If you

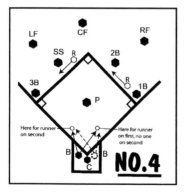

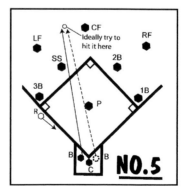

have a runner on third with less than 2 outs, have them hit the ball as hard and as far as they can for a *"sacrifice fly" (NO.5)*.

Bunting for a hit (NO.6)

Some of time you may just want to get your players on base against a tough pitcher any way you can. Bunting for a hit can accomplish this. Surprise is your advantage. To bunt for a hit have your batters do two things. They should be in motion just as the bat makes contact, and they need to grip the bat more firmly. For right handers, push or dump the ball past the pitcher and between first and second. For left handers, drag bunt the ball or just tap the ball down the third base line.

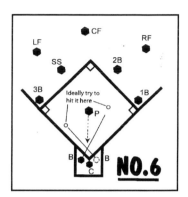

Stealing Bases (NO.7)

Steals are a good way to get your players into scoring position. Two good ones are the *delayed* steal and the *double* steal. For the *delayed* steal have your runner slide step out into their leadoff. Then as the pitcher releases the ball towards the batter, have them count slowly 1-2-3 then make a fast break to the next base. You can also have them pretend to go back to the base then whirl around and break for the next base. This will usually catch the catcher off guard. Also on steals to second there will be times when the catcher gets rattled and in a hurry then throws down to second, but no one is there covering

Double steals are possible when you have runners on first and second. Make sure your runners know they have to execute this play simultaneously. When there are no outs is a good time. The catcher can't throw them both out at once.

On steals tell your players to hook slide away from the side of the base the infielder is on. If the infielder is straddling the base tell your players to slide straight in, with their shoe sole parallel to the base edge and both arms and hands thrown way back behind them.

11

Squeeze Play (NO.8)

Squeeze plays are usually used in a low scoring tight game, with less than two outs, and when one run might make the difference. There are 3 basic types. The "regular squeeze", the "safety squeeze", and the "suicide squeeze".

The *regular squeeze* is just a sacrifice bunt where your batter bunts between the pitcher and first base. The runner has a leadoff then breaks for home when they see the bunt will not be easily caught. If they get thrown out at first the run scores and they have done their job.

The *safety squeeze* is when the runner on third takes their leadoff, holds, and only breaks for home when they see the batter make contact and the bunt is going to be away from an infielder. If it looks like the infielder will quickly get to the ball and field it, the runner goes back to third base.

The *suicide squeeze* is more risky. Your runner has to take their leadoff then break for home plate just as the ball leaves the pitchers hand. The other forgotten part of the play is the runner has to make a great slide. When the play is called make sure your runners know they have to break for home on the next pitch no matter what happens.

Have them slide according to where the catcher is located. If the catcher blocks the plate standing up, make sure you show your players how to throw a shoulder block on them and try to make them drop the ball. If the catcher is out in front of the plate have them hook slide from behind the plate. If the catcher is behind the plate have them hook slide to the infield side.

There can be no delays or going back to third. The batter has to bunt or make contact with the pitch even if it is a little out of their reach or the strike zone. If the batter does not swing, or misses the pitch, the catcher is going to be right there to tag the runner out. This is why it is called a "suicide squeeze".

All your batter has to do is bunt the ball on the ground in fair territory. If your batter bunts it foul with less than two strikes, the worst that can happen is your runner has to go back to third.

Defensive Plays

There are a number of defensive plays your players need to know. These are plays they need to know and execute when they are out in the field.

Simple Basic Defensive Plays

Pick-off Plays

There are pick-off plays for all three bases. And on first and second there are several different kinds.

First Base Pick-offs (NO.9)

There are several basic ways to pick-off runners at first base. The most common way is when the pitcher uses deception to catch the runner too far off base, leaning the wrong way, or not paying attention. When you are facing a team without very good players or coaching, it's a little easier to fool the runner. Down at the lower levels I like the pitcher and catcher having signs.

Pitcher Variation

The catcher watches the runner while the pitcher appears to not be paying attention to the runner (does not even look over). This will give cocky runners a false sense of safety. Then just at the moment the runner gets too far away, or is not paying attention, the catcher signals the pitcher who immediately whirls around quickly and throws over to the first baseman.

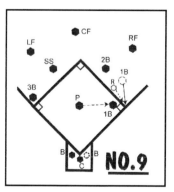

First Baseman Variation

The first baseman does not hold the runner on, instead they play back a little just behind the runner when they take their leadoff. This does several things. It makes good players nervous who don't see this too often. And it gives inexperienced runners a false sense of safety. How it works is the catcher signals the pitcher the minute the first baseman breaks for the bag. The pitcher whirls and throws over immediately after getting the sign.

Catcher Variations

Variation 1 has the catcher setting it up. He signals the pitcher and first baseman that the play is on. They both have to acknowledge by returning a signal. Then the catcher gives them a second signal. After the second signal they both count by 1000's. The first baseman breaks for the bag at 1003, then the pitcher whirls and throws over on 1004 with the first baseman and the ball getting there at the same time. Depending on the age and speed of the players you may have to adjust the timing on this play.

Variation 2 has the catcher noticing the runner on first takes their time going back to the base after a pitch, They signal the first baseman that the play is on. The first baseman has to acknowledge back. On the very next pitch the catcher pops up and throws down to first base. Then just as the pitch gets to the catcher, the first baseman breaks quickly to the bag. You may have to make adjustments here also to get the timing down.

All these plays are based on precise timing and signaling. You will have to practice this a lot to get them to work. It took me 2-3 years of working with young players 7-9 years old to get this play down. Also make sure your pitchers all know that when their foot is not on the rubber, or they step backwards off the rubber, they can throw over or fake a throw over at any time without a balk being called.

Second Base Pick-offs (NO.10)

There are several basic ways to pick-off runners at second base. The most common way is when the pitcher uses deception to catch the runner off base. There are two basic plays the *daylight play*, and *the timing play.*

Daylight play

How it works is the pitcher whirls and throws right at second base, about belt high, as soon as they look over and see a large space (the daylight) between the runner and the breaking shortstop. It's the shortstops job to get over to the base on time for the throw. Your center fielder has to back up the play in case of a throw that gets away into the outfield.

14

This can also be worked with the second baseman if they are covering. It's a little harder though because the runner can usually see the second baseman sneaking in out of the corner of their eye. This can work if you notice the runner has a bad habit of looking over their right shoulder at the shortstop. But it works best with the shortstop.

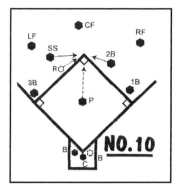

A *TIP* here. Watch out though because this play can backfire if the shortstop is just faking the runner to hold them closer to the base by pretending to sneak over to second behind them. This can confuse young pitchers as to when to throw over thinking the play is on. Then they throw it away.

Timing play

How it works is the pitcher looks at the player covering second and signals them before looking back at the catcher. Then as the pitcher looks back at home plate, just at that moment both players start counting by 1000's. On "1003" the player covering second breaks quickly for the bag. On "1004" the pitcher spins and throws right at second about belt high. If the player covering second is positioned right they should arrive at second at the same time as the throw.

Pitchouts

Runner on first only *(NO.11)*

When the count is favorable, with the count of one ball or less, you can call a pitchout. This is used when you are pretty sure the runner on first likes to steal and is wandering way off base (most common play). The catcher gives your pitcher the signal. Then just as the pitcher starts the pitch to the plate, the catcher steps over into the box opposite the batter.

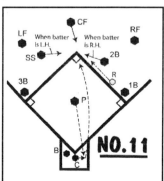

Then knowing the *pitchout* sign is on, the pitcher will throw way outside to the catcher preferably at letter height. The catcher should immediately stand upright and make the throw down to second. If it's a R.H. batter 2B covers. If it's a L.H. batter SS covers. If the runner gets halfway down, can see they won't make it, then tries to get back to first you get them in a rundown (hot box). For the different *rundown* situations *SEE NOS. 13, 14, 15, 16.*

Runner on second, or first & second *(NO.12)*

A runner stealing third base is not too common. When they do your catcher has to be ready. It works the same as when the runner is on

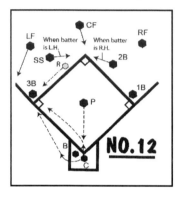

first except when it's a right handed batter (most of the time) the catcher has to quickly jump out in front of the batter.

This so that the batter can not obstruct the catchers view or their throw down to third. Also the left fielder and center fielder have to come in and back up their base in case the throw gets away from the third baseman.

Run-Downs Plays (Hot Box)

Rundowns usually happen when a pick-off play catches or traps a runner between two bases. Each situation requires a little different play by the infielders. While tossing the ball to each other you chase the runner back and forth until he can be tagged. The more throws your player make though the more chance one of them will throw the ball away. Players make as few throws as possible.

Here are the basic rules on how to do it effectively.

■ After the run-down starts make sure your players understand that they have to chase the runner back towards the base they just left.

■ The fielder with the ball holds it high and away from his glove so that the other players can see it.

■ Whoever is waiting to receive the throw gives the player with the ball a target to throw to.

16

- When a right hand throwing player is chasing the runner back to a team mate at second, the team mate stands to their left of the incoming runner. This gives the thrower a clear view of their target glove. Also this way the throw is less likely to hit the runner.
- If the thrower is left handed the receiving team mate stands to the right of the incoming runner.
- During rundowns make sure your players stay out of the base line while waiting for the throw so that obstruction is not called.
- Don't fake a throw during the run-down. It might also fake out a team mate waiting to receive the ball.
- Hold the ball high so the team mate can see it. Only cock the arm back when getting ready to release the ball.
- When not involved in the run-down, choose an unoccupied base to back up the play. Player should stay out of the way unless the play comes in their direction.

Runners on First & Second, Runner on First Picked Off (NO.13)

1) **First Baseman** is tag man with ball. Also covers first without the ball. 2) **Pitcher** backs up First. 3) **Catcher** covers home plate. 4) **Second Baseman** is the run-down player. Also covers second base. 5) **Shortstop** Backs up and covers second base, with a possibility of being the run-down player and tagger. 6) **Third Baseman** covers third to keep runner on second from advancing. 7) **Right Fielder** comes in to help back up first base. 8) **Center** and **Left Fielder** come in to help back up second base.

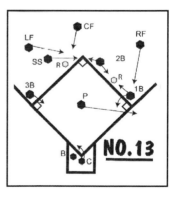

Runners on First & Second, Runner on second Picked Off (NO.14)

1) **First Baseman** covers first base. 2) **Pitcher** backs up third. 3) **Catcher** covers home plate. 4) **Second Baseman** covers second base, with the possibility of being the run-down player.

17

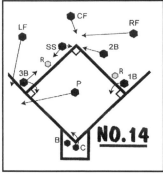

5) **Shortstop** is the tag man with the ball. Also covers second base without the ball. 6) **Third Baseman** is the run-down player. Also covers third base. 7) **Right** and **Center Fielders** back up second base.

8) **Left Fielder** moves to help back up and cover third base.

Runners on First & Third, Runner on Third Picked Off (NO.15)

1) **First Baseman** covers first to keep runner from advancing. 2) **Pitcher** backs up catcher and covers home plate 3)

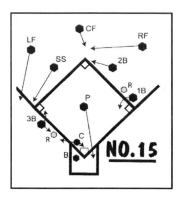

Catcher is the run-down man, and covers home plate. 4) **Second Baseman** covers second base to keep the runner on first from advancing. 5) **Shortstop** backs up third baseman 6) **Third Baseman** is the tag man with the ball. Also covers third base 7) **Right** and **Center Fielders** come in to help back up second base. 8) **Left Fielder** moves behind third to help back up third base.

Runner on Third Tries to Score on Ground Ball with Infield Pulled In, Runner gets Trapped Between Bases (NO.16)

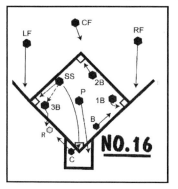

1) **First Baseman** covers first. 2) **Pitcher** backs up catcher and covers home plate 3) **Catcher** is the run-down man, and covers home plate. 4) **Second Baseman** covers second base to keep a runner on first from advancing. 5) **Shortstop** backs up third baseman 6) **Third Baseman** is the tag man with the ball. Also covers third base 7) **Right Fielder**

backs up first base. 8) **Center Fielder** backs up second base. 9) **Left Fielder** moves behind third to help back up third base.

Double Plays

There are a number of ways to turn a double play. Since making most double plays happen at second base, we will talk a little more about that location. Here are some key *TIPS* or techniques to teach your Second Basemen and Shortstops:

- *Very Important.* Tell your players to take time enough make that first throw or flip toss a good one. Don't hurry and make an error or they may not get anybody out.
- Also have them make sure to make their throws to the first and second without hitting the runner from in front or in back.
- For them to get something on their throws, have them turn their right foot toward first base as they set it across and in front of the bag.
- Have them use a smaller glove so that they can get rid of the ball more quickly.
- Have them make sure to keep both hands together to get rid of the ball. This saves time.
- Explain to them not to feel like *every* ball hit to them, with a man on first, is a double play. The speed and direction of the ball coming at them determines this.
- Have them think always get the lead runner. Their job is catch the ball first, then give the receiving player a good throw.
- Your Shortstop should take all throws from balls hit back to the pitcher unless a known R.H. pull hitter is at the plate. Then the Second Baseman takes the throw. They have to let each other know who is covering.
- If your Shortstop has a weak arm though your Second Baseman should take all the throws.
- When going to the bag to execute the play, that player has to *charge* the bag hard, then has a slight hesitation or shuffle to see what direction the throw is coming from. When the player making the throw to them is closer they can anticipate

a good throw. The farther they are away, the more they have to ready to handle a bad throw.

- When they receive a poor throw on their glove side, it may be necessary to throw their left leg to the left and tag the bag with their right foot, throwing as the right foot touches the bag.
- Tell them when at all possible come across the bag to get out of the way of the runner.
- Have them use the corners and side of the bag as a pushing off point so that they don't trip or stumble on the high part of the bag.
- Have them learn to determine their distance from the bag when fielding the ball, then decide quickly whether to throw or underhand toss the ball.
- When making an underhand shovel toss, have them learn to give it firmly to their team mate covering, and with no spin. Keeping their wrist stiff increases accuracy.
- Tell them when the ball is hit close enough to the bag, then tag the bag themselves. When not necessary don't handle the ball twice (throwing it). Tell them if they can to stay in back of the bag.
- Tell them not to hide their throws. There is maybe only one time they will turn completely around, and that is when the ball is hit deep in the hole. And that catch will be very difficult to make to start the double play.
- Tell them that most of the time there is no need to jump or make a full pivot on the double play. Just catch the throw, turn their hips and upper part of their body, bring their hands and the ball back, and throw.
- For them to find the amount of ground they can cover, during practice draw a line in the infield. On one side of the line they must throw, on the other side they can shovel toss.

Runner on First 3-6-3 First-to Short-to First Double Play (NO. 17)

1) Right handed **First Baseman** catches ground ball, quickly turns clockwise to throw to the shortstop if the ball is hit right at them. If it is hit to their left, they will probably have to turn counterclockwise before throwing. Left handed **First Baseman**

pivots clockwise to their glove side to make their throw. Then immediately go back to the bag for the return throw. 2) **Shortstop** breaks for second when they see hit is going to the first baseman. They tag the bag (force out) and throw back to first. They have to make sure they make a good throw. They should not worry about getting hit by the runner. 3) **First Baseman** gets ready to stretch out and catch the return throw to complete the play.

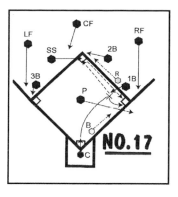

Runner on First 3-4-3 First-to Second- to First Double Play (NO. 18)

1) Right handed **First Baseman** catches ball, turns clockwise to throw to the shortstop if the ball is hit right at them. If it is hit to their left, they will probably have to turn counterclockwise before throwing. Left handed **First Baseman** pivots clockwise to their glove side to make their throw. Then immediately go back to the bag for the return throw. 2) **Second Baseman** breaks for second when they see hit is going to the first baseman. They tag the bag (force out) and throw back to first. They have to make sure they make a good throw. They should not worry about getting hit by the runner. 3) **First Baseman** gets ready to stretch out and catch the return throw to complete the play.

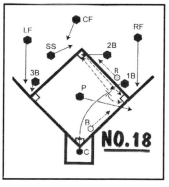

Runner on First 6-4-3 Short- to Second- to First Double Play (NO. 19) Most Common. Make sure they learn this one.

1) Right handed **Shortstop** catches ball, plants their right foot, then quickly turns counterclockwise to throw side arm to second if the ball is hit to their right or right at them. If it is hit to their left, they will have to make the catch, quickly come under control,

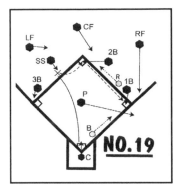

NO.19

probably have to underhand scoop, or back hand, the ball to the second baseman while on the run. Left handed **Shortstops** kind of reverse what a right hander does to make their throws. They should also cheat a little closer to second when the possibility of a double play is in order. 2) **Second Baseman** breaks for second when they see hit is going to the shortstop. They tag the bag (force out), get out of the way of the runner coming in, and throw to first. They should not worry about getting hit by the runner, just get a good throw off. 3) **First Baseman** breaks to the bag when they see that the ball is hit to short. Then they get in position, and stretch out to catch the second baseman's throw to complete the play.

Runner on First 5-4-3 Third- to Second- to First Double Play (NO. 20) *Third Most Common. Make sure they learn this one.*

1) Right handed **Third baseman** catches ball, plants their right foot, then quickly turns counterclockwise to make a strong side arm throw to the second baseman if the ball is hit to their right

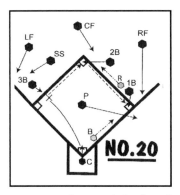

NO.20

or right at them. If it is hit just a little to their left they should drop the left foot back a little, and open up their body. If it is hit to farther their left, or a slow roller, they will have to make the catch on the run, quickly come under control while moving, and side arm throw to the second baseman while on the run. Maybe even pick up the ball with their right hand. Left handed **Third Baseman** kind of reverse what a right hander does to make their throws. Third baseman should also not play too deep in the hole when the possibility of a double play is in order. Since the throw to second is going to be a hard throw, the center fielder has to make sure to swing around to be in position for an overthrow. 2) **Second Baseman** breaks for second when they see hit is going to the third baseman. They tag the bag (force out), get out of the way of the runner coming in, and throw to first. They should not worry about getting hit by the runner, just get a good throw off. 3) **First Baseman** breaks to the bag when they see that the ball is hit to third. Then they get in position, and stretch out to catch the second baseman's throw to complete the play. Since all the throws are going to be long and hurried, the pitcher and right fielder need to be in position for any overthrows to first.

Runner on First 4-6-3 Second- to Short- to First Double Play (NO. 21) Second Most Common. *Make sure they learn this one.*

1) Right handed **Second Baseman** catches ball, plants their right foot, then quickly turns clockwise to throw underhand scoop, or back hand, the ball to the shortstop if the ball is hit to their right or right at them. If it is hit to their left, they will have to make the catch, quickly come under control, and probably have to side arm to the second baseman while on the move. Left handed **Second Baseman** kind of reverses what a right hander does to make their throws. Both should also cheat a little closer to second when there is a double play possibility. 2) **Shortstop** breaks for second

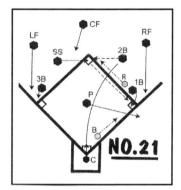

when they see hit is going to the second baseman. They tag the bag (force out), get out of the way of the runner coming in, and throw to first. They should not worry about getting hit by the runner, just getting a good throw off is their priority. 3) **First Baseman** breaks to the bag when they see that the ball is hit to second. Then they get in position, and stretch out to catch the second baseman's throw to complete the play.

Runner on First 1-6-3 Pitcher- to Short- to First Double Play (NO. 22)

1) Right handed **Pitcher** catches ball, plants their left foot, pivots on it, steps toward second with it as they quickly turn clockwise to throw side arm (quickest) to the second baseman covering if the

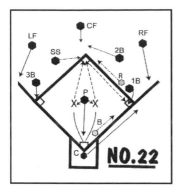

ball is hit a little to their right or right at them. If it is hit to their left, they will have to plant their left foot, swing around to their left counterclockwise, face second base (get the lead runner), and side arm a throw to the shortstop covering. Make sure your pitchers ask or signal and always know who is covering second base when there is a double play possibility. Left handed **Pitchers** will have to reverse their pivots and turns to throw to second. Who covers second will depend on RH or LH batter or your choice depending on the batter. 2) **Shortstop** breaks for second when they see hit is going to the pitcher. They tag the bag (force out), get out of the way of the runner coming in, and throw to first. They should not worry about getting hit by the runner, just get a good throw off is their priority. 3) **First Baseman** breaks to the bag when they see that the ball is hit to pitcher. Then they get in position, and stretch out to catch the shortstops throw to complete the play.

Runner on First 1-4-3 Pitcher- to Second- to First Double Play (No.23)

1) Right handed **Pitcher** catches ball, plants their left foot, pivots on it, steps toward second with it as they quickly turn clockwise

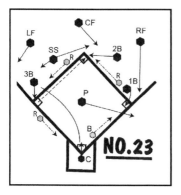

to throw side arm (quickest) to the second baseman covering, when the ball is hit a little to their right or right at them. If it is hit to their left though they will have to plant their left foot, swing around to their left counterclockwise, face second base (get the lead runner), and side arm a throw to the shortstop covering. Make sure your pitchers ask or signal and always know who is covering second base when there is a double play possibility. Left handed **Pitchers** will have to reverse their pivots and turns to throw to second. Who covers second will depend on RH or LH batter or your choice depending on the batter. 2) **Second Baseman** breaks for second when they see hit is going to the pitcher. They tag the bag (force out), get out of the way of the runner coming in, and throw to first. They should not worry about getting hit by the runner, just get a good throw off is their priority. 3) **First Baseman** breaks to the bag when they see that the ball is hit to pitcher. Then they get in position, and stretch out to catch the second baseman's throw to complete the play.

Runners on First & Second or Bases Loaded 5-4 Third- to Second Double Play (NO. 24)

1) **Third Baseman** catches ball when they are close to the bag and ground ball is right to them, takes it to the bag, tags the bag for one, then throws down to the second baseman covering second. 2) **Second Baseman** breaks for the bag when they see the ball is going to the third. They take the throw, tag the bag, come across it towards third, and get out of the way of the runner coming in to complete the play.

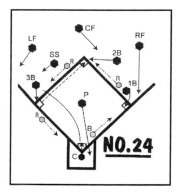

Bases Loaded 5-2 Third- to Catcher Double Play (NO. 25)

1) **Third Baseman** catches ball when they are close to the bag and ground ball is right to them, takes it to the bag, tags the bag for one, keeps coming across the bag, then throws home to the catcher covering the plate 2) **Catcher** gets out in front of the third base side of the plate when they see the ball is going to the third and the runner is coming. They take the throw, then tag the bag for the force out to complete the play. Make sure your pitchers know they have to back up the catcher on this play in case of an over throw. I like this play better

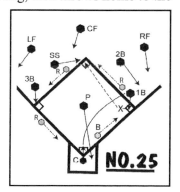

than No.24 if your third baseman can quickly get to the bag because their motion in already coming to the plate.

Runner on First, First & Second, or Bases Loaded 3-6 First- to First- to Second Double Play (NO. 26)

Use this play when there is already one out so that one or more runs can't score on bases loaded.

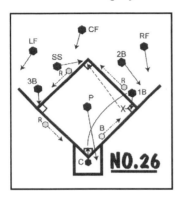

1) **First Baseman** catches ball when they are close to the bag and ground ball is right to them, takes it to the bag, tags the bag for one, keeps coming across the bag, pivots then throws down to the shortstop covering second. 2) **Shortstop** quickly moves to second when they see the ball is going to the first baseman. They take the throw, then tag the bag for the force out to complete the play. Then they keep moving across the bag and stay out of the way of the runner coming in. Make sure your outfielders properly back up and cover their bases on this play in case of an over throw.

Runner on First, First & Second, or Bases Loaded 6-3 Shortstop- to First Double Play (NO. 27)

Use this play when there is already one out so that one or more runs can't score on bases loaded.

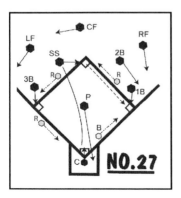

1) **Shortstop** catches ball when they are close to the bag and ground ball is right to them, takes it quickly to the bag, tags the bag for one, keeps coming across the bag, pivots then throws down to the first baseman. 2) **First Baseman** quickly moves to first base when they see the ball is going to the shortstop. They take the throw, then tag the bag for the force out to complete the play.

Then they keep moving across the bag and stay out of the way of the runner coming in. Make sure your outfielders properly back up and cover their bases on this play in case of an over throw.

Runner on First, First & Second, or Bases Loaded 4-3 Second-to First Double Play (NO. 28)

Use this play when there is already one out so that one or more runs can't score on bases loaded.

1) **Second Baseman** catches ball when they are close to the bag and ground ball is right to them, takes it quickly to the bag, tags the bag for one, keeps coming across the bag, pivots then throws down to the first baseman.

2) **First Baseman** quickly moves to first base when they see the ball is going to the second baseman. They take the throw, then tag the bag to complete the play. Then they keep moving across the bag and stay out of the way of the runner coming in. Make sure your outfielders and infielders properly back up and cover their bases on this play in case of an over throw.

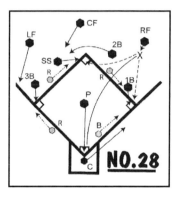

NOTE:

The following are plays where your first baseman goes into the infield for a bunt or a slow roller, and another player has to cover first base.

Runners on First, First & Second, or Bases Loaded 3-6-1 First-to Short- to Pitcher Covering Double Play (NO. 29)

Use this play when there is already one out so that one or more runs can't score on bases loaded.

1) **First Baseman** moves into the infield for a bunt or slow roller when they are close to the bag and the ball is hit right at them. They pivot and throw to the shortstop covering second for one out.

2) **Shortstop** quickly moves to second for the throw when they see the ball is going to the first baseman, takes the throw, tags the bag,

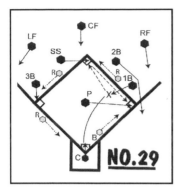

throws over to first, then gets out of the way of the runner coming in.

3) **Pitcher** quickly moves over to cover first when they see that the first baseman will get to ball first. They take the throw from the shortstop, and tag first base for the out on the batter to complete the play.

Runners on First, First & Second, or Bases Loaded 3-6-4 First- to Short- to Second Baseman Covering Double Play (NO. 30)

Use this play when there is already one out so that one or more runs can't score on bases loaded.

1) **First Baseman** moves into the infield for a bunt or slow roller when they see that the pitcher won't get to it. They make the catch, pivot and throw to the shortstop covering second for one out.

2) **Shortstop** quickly moves to second for the throw when they see the ball is going to the first baseman, takes the throw, tags the bag,

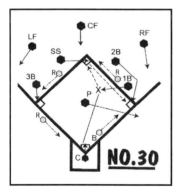

throws over to first, then gets out of the way of the runner coming in.

3) **Second Baseman** very quickly moves over to cover first when they see the ball is going to the first baseman and the pitcher is out of position, or is not going to be able to cover first. They take the throw from the shortstop, and tag first base for the out on the batter to complete the play.

NOTE:

These are plays involving the catcher and pitcher in the double play. Some are referred to as, "strike-em Out-throw-em-out".

Runner on First,1-2-4 Pitcher- to Catcher- to Second Baseman Covering Double Play (NO.31)

Use this play when there is only a runner on first. It's risky with young kids when there is runners at first & second, or bases loaded.

1) **Pitcher** has two strikes on the batter and can see that the runner on first is looking to steal. Or the hit and run may be on. This is when your pitcher wants to get a strike out. So they throw hard and try for the strike out. 2) **Catcher** can see the runner wants to go, so they get ready to pop up throwing. The pitcher gets the strike out, the catcher comes up and guns a throw down to

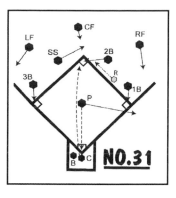

the second baseman covering. The player covering needs to straddle the bag, move up a little towards first, then put a tag on the runner trying to slide in.

3) **Second Baseman** usually covers because the batter is usually right handed. The shortstop stays at short in case the batter hits the ball towards short. Usually in this situation, when the batter is left handed though the shortstop covers in case the batter hits it towards second. When the shortstop covers second, it's a "1-2-6" double play.

Runner on Third 1-2-5 Pitcher- to Catcher- to Third Baseman Covering Double Play (NO.32)

Use this play when there is only a runner on third, they are taking a big lead off, and there is already one out. It's risky with young kids when there is bases loaded and no one out because the catcher might throw it away out into left field and a lot of runs will score.

1) **Pitcher** has two strikes on the batter and can see that the runner on third is taking a big lead off in a tight game. Or the Squeeze play might be on. This is when your pitcher wants to get a strike out. So they throw hard and try for the strike out. 2) **Catcher** can see the runner wants to go, so they get ready to pop up and throw. The pitcher gets the strike out, the catcher comes up, catches the runner way off base, and

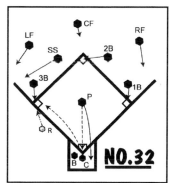

guns a throw down to the third baseman covering. The player covering needs to straddle the bag, move up a little towards home plate, then put a tag on the runner attempting to get back or slide into the bag.

Now if the runner turns around and heads for home, the third baseman and the catcher get them in a rundown, and tag them for the second out.

NOTE:

Here is a rare play involving the catcher and first baseman. However, it can get you a double play.

Bases Loaded 3-2-3 First- to Home- Back to First Baseman Covering Double Play (NO.33)

This is a rare play for young kids, but only use it when there is a runner on third that is forced to run to home plate on a hit. It's a tight game, you don't want the run to score, so you go for the lead runner. If there is already one out, you are out of the inning.

1) **First Baseman** catches a slow grounder or hard bunt right to them. Knowing that keeping the run from scoring is important has them quickly coming up throwing

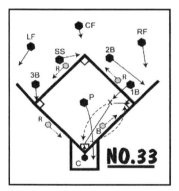

to the catcher, for the force out at the plate. 2) **Catcher** comes up, gets out in front of the plate, takes the throw, tags the plate, and immediately fires the ball back to the first baseman to get the batter. 3) **First Baseman** quickly gets back to first, touches the bag, then stretches out towards the catcher to get the incoming batter for the second out.

This works quite well when you can determine that the batter is a slow runner.

NOTE:

These are unassisted plays where the runner gets doubled off base when the infielder catches a line drive then quickly runs over and tags the bag. This happens mostly with second base or shortstop, but it can happen at first or third.

30

Runner on Second, or Bases Loaded 6-6 or 4-4 Shortstop or Second Baseman Unassisted Double Play (NO.34)

1) **Shortstop** is cheating a little closer to second when batter hits a line drive right at them, which they catch for one out. The runner gets caught off base. Shortstop runs quickly over and tags the base for out two (6-6) before the runner can get back. When it is bases loaded, and they accidentally drop the line drive, all they have to do is tag the base for the force out on the runner coming in, then throw to first.

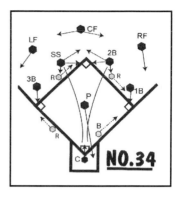

There is a variation of this where the shortstop catches the line drive, then just runs right at the runner trying to get back and tags them out.

2. When the line drive is caught by the **Second Baseman** they either tag the base or the runner, just like the shortstop, and it becomes a 4-4 unassisted double play.

Runner on First or Third, or Bases Loaded 3-3 or 5-5 First or Third Baseman Unassisted Double Play (NO.35)

1) **First or Third Baseman** is cheating a little closer to their base when batter hits a line drive right at them, which they catch for one out. The runner gets caught off base. They run quickly over and tag the base for out two before the runner can get back.

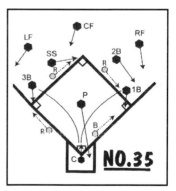

There is a variation of this also where they catch the line drive, then just runs right at the runner trying to get back and tags them out.

These are BANG-BANG (quick) plays that can get you out of the inning very quickly if there is already one out. Also teach your players to be careful to make sure they catch the line drive first, then look for the base or runner. If they don't get their runner for some reason, make sure they learn to quickly check the other bases for possibilities.

NOTE:

This is a rare case where the first or third baseman are playing in at cutoff depth, and a line drive or a nubber is hit in the air right to them. They catch the ball then double off a runner trying to get back to their base.

Runner on Second, or Bases Loaded 3-6 or 5-6 First or Third- to Shortstop Double Play (NO.36)

1) **First or Third Baseman** is playing in at cutoff depth.

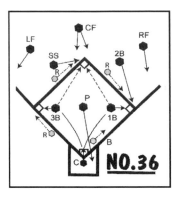

The ball is hit right at them in the air for one out. Then they whirl and turn towards second, and fire the ball down to the shortstop covering second. 2. **Shortstop** can see that the first or third baseman has caught the ball and they quickly break for second. Then they take the throw and tag the base or the runner for out number two.

Outfield Numbering

I am going to go over outfield double plays here, so I am going to give the players numbers to help describe the plays. Left Field will be **No.7**, Center Field will be **No.8**, and Right Field will be **No.9** (this numbering is pretty common). This play can work on any base where the runner can be doubled off, but usually happens at first or second. In youth baseball the center fielder usually plays deep to keep hits from getting by them. This usually keeps them too deep to come in for line drives. However, on a rare occasion they could be playing in close for a weak batter. In that case you could have an 8-6, 8-4, 8-1, or 8-5 double play

Runners on Second or Third, or Bases Loaded 7-4 or 7-5 Left Field- to Second or Third Double Play (NO.37)

1) **Left Fielder** comes in fast and catches a low line drive either by a shoe top catch or sliding on their stomach. The runners are usually taught to go half way to the next base and watch the ball. When it looks like the outfielder won't make the catch, some young runners will hesitate, or start towards the next base.

Then when the outfielder makes a great catch and comes up throwing behind the runner, they get picked off trying to get back to the base, and it results in a double play.

2. **Second Baseman** who is normally covering when the hit goes to the other side, can see that the left fielder has caught the ball and they quickly break for second. Then they take the throw and tag the base or

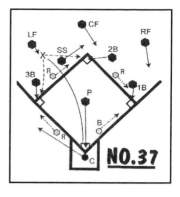

the runner for out number two. The same play can go to the **Third Baseman** depending on which runner the left fielder thinks they can best double off the base.

Runners on First or Second, or Bases Loaded 9-1 or 9-6 Right Field- to First or Second Double Play (NO.38)

1) **Right Fielder** comes in fast and catches a low line drive either by a shoe top catch or sliding on their stomach. The runners are usually taught to go half way to the next base and watch the ball. When it looks like the outfielder won't make the catch, some young runners will hesitate.

Then when the outfielder makes a great catch and comes up throwing behind the runner, they get picked off trying to get back to the base, and it results in a double play.

2. **First Baseman** who is normally covering when the hit goes to the outfield, can see that the right fielder has caught the ball and they quickly break for first. Then they take the throw and tag the base or the runner for out number two. The same play can go to the **Shortstop** depending on which runner the right fielder thinks they can best double off the base.

NOTE:

There are some additional outfield double plays that can be made at the youth level although they are pretty rare. These are when a fly ball is hit into the outfield, then caught by an outfielder and fired in to the catcher at home plate.

Runners on First, or Second, or on Third, or Bases Loaded 7-2, 8-2, 9-2 Outfielder- to Catcher Double Play (NO.39)

1) **Left, Center, or Right Fielder** circles under a fly ball, gets set, makes the catch for one out, and immediately throws a one bounce throw to the catcher at home plate.

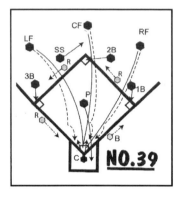

The reason this does not happen to often in the lower youth baseball divisions is because most young outfielders usually don't have a strong enough arm and an accurate throw. 2) **Catcher** comes out in front of the plate just a little up the base line, and faces the outfielder making the throw. If they are going to block the plate, make sure you tell them to get set because the runner will try to knock them down and cause them to drop the ball.

Also make sure they understand they can not block the plate or base line and interfere with the runner unless the ball is in their glove or almost to them. And they have to tag the runner in most cases. For the real little kids I like to have them get close to the base line on the infield side, then tag them as they go by for out two. Many times the runner coming in will come in standing up because they think they won't have to slide, or they can make it without being tagged.

NOTE:

There are several bad bunt plays that can result in a double play. When I say bad bunt, I mean a but that goes right to a charging pitcher, first baseman, or third baseman. Or a bunt not too far away, right out in front of the plate where a catcher can get to it quickly.

Runner on First 2-4-3 or 2-6-3 Catcher- to Second- to First Double Play (NO.40)

1) **Catcher** fields a bunt right out in front of the plate on either the left or right side of the infield. Picks it up quickly and guns a throw down to the second baseman or shortstop covering for out one. 2) **Second Baseman** is covering second when bunt goes to the left side of infield. **Shortstop** covers second when bunt goes to the right side of infield. They break for the base as soon as they see the catcher is going to field the bunt. They take the throw, tag the base, come across the bag to get out of the way of the runner, and throw over to first. 3) **First Baseman** already

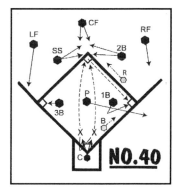

playing in at cutoff depth, starts to come in for the bunt. As soon as they see that the catcher has it, they quickly get back to first for the second baseman's or shortstops throw over for out number two.

Runner on First 3-6-4 or 5-4-3 First or Third- to Second or Short- to First Double Play (NO.41)

1) **First Baseman or Third Baseman** comes in, fields the bunt, pivots, turns, and throws down to the shortstop or second baseman covering second for out number one. 2) **Shortstop** is covering second when bunt goes to the right side of infield. **Second Baseman** covers second when bunt goes to the left side of infield. They break for the base as soon as they see the first baseman or third baseman is going to field the bunt. They take the throw, tag the base, come across the bag to get out of the way of the runner, and throw over to first. 3) **Second Baseman** covers first when the first baseman moves in to field the bunt. They get in position, stretch out, and get ready to take the throw from second. **First Baseman** starts in then goes back to

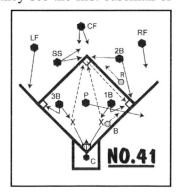

35

first when they see that the third baseman will field the bunt. They stretch out and take the throw for out two.

Runner on First 1-4-3 or 1-6-3 Pitcher- to Second or Short- to First Double Play (NO.42)

1) **Pitcher** comes in, fields the bunt, pivots, turns, and throws down to the shortstop or second baseman covering second for out

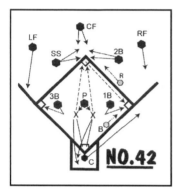

number one. 2) **Shortstop** is covering second when bunt goes to the right side of infield. **Second Baseman** covers second when bunt goes to the left side of infield. They break for the base as soon as they see the pitcher is going to field the bunt. They take the throw, tag the base, come across the bag to get out of the way of the runner, and throw over to first. 3) **First Baseman** starts in then goes back to first when they see that the pitcher will field the bunt. They stretch out and take the throw from second base for out number two.

NOTE:

What if it's a tight game and the opposing team decides to "Squeeze" or "Suicide Squeeze" against you. Wouldn't it be nice to get a double play, especially if there is already one out. Here are some plays you can try, especially if you have good fielding infielders on the corners and at pitcher. Have your first and third baseman come in to *cutoff depth*.

Runner on Third 1-5-4 or 3-5-4 Pitcher or First Baseman- to Third Baseman- to First Double Play (NO.43)

1) **Pitcher** and **First Baseman** charge in fast as soon as the batter squares for bunt. Whichever player fields the bunt throws quickly over to the third baseman who tags the runner. This play is based on players being told to bunt to the right side of the infield on squeeze plays. 2) This leaves the **Third Baseman** open to dog the runner close and just behind them up and down the line. Then when

they get the ball they just reach over and tag the runner, then quickly throw over to the second baseman covering first. 3) **Second Baseman** covers first when bunt goes to the right side of infield. They break for first base as soon as they see the pitcher or first baseman is going to field the bunt. They touch the bag with their foot, face the third baseman, take the throw, then pull their foot off the bag to get out of the way of the runner coming in. This is out two.

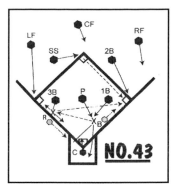

NOTE:
This is one of the more conventional plays for squeeze bunts, either suicide or safety.

Runner on Third 2-4-2 Catcher- to First- Back to Catcher Double Play (NO.44)

1) **Catcher** throws off their mask, charges out fast as soon as the batter bunts out in front of the plate. They look at the runner coming in from third, if the runner stops, they fake them into going back towards third. Then they whirl and gun a throw down to the second baseman covering first for out one. Then they immediately go back to the plate for a return throw from first.

2) **Second Baseman** covering on the play breaks for first as soon as they see the catcher is fielding the bunt. They take the throw touch the bag with their foot, come across the bag towards home plate, and gun a throw back to the catcher at home plate. The **Catcher** takes the

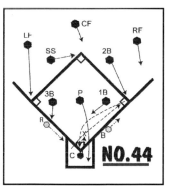

throw, then tags the runner coming in. If your catcher is tough, have them take a peak, and if the runner is coming they can block the plate. To keep the runner back closer to third, have the third baseman dog them close so that they can't sneak in before the return throw.

NOTE:

This is a very uncommon defensive plays for squeeze bunts, either suicide or safety. One coach used this because he got so tired of other teams squeezing in runs on his team in low run tight situations. I think you only want to set this play up when you are desperate and absolutely need to stop the squeeze when you are pretty sure it is on.

Runner on Third 9-3-2, 9-3, or 9-2-3 Outfielder- to First or Catcher, or back to First Double Play (NO.45)

1) The **Right Fielder** (or your slowest foot speed outfielder) is brought in and locates right in front of the pitcher just off to the side depending on if the pitcher is a right hander or a left hander. When the batter bunts the outfielder goes to the ball and fields it. Every one else on the infield is in on the grass at cutoff depth to guard against a slow roller past the outfielder.

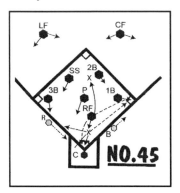

When the outfielder fields the ball they check the runner at third. If the runner stays at third, they throw to first base to get batter. If the runner (lead runner) is coming home they either run right at them and tag them or they throw to the catcher for the tag. After the tag is made they throw to first for out number two.

If the batter picks up two strikes during the at bat, the outfielder will reposition behind the mound to guard against a ground ball up the middle.

2) **First Baseman** covering on the play breaks for first as soon as they see the outfielder is fielding the bunt. They take the throw touch the bag with their foot, then pivot, turn towards home plate, and gun a throw back to the catcher at home plate. The **Catcher** takes the throw, then tags the runner coming in. If your catcher is tough, have them take a peak, and if the runner is coming they can block the plate if they get the ball. To keep the runner back closer to third, have the third baseman dog them close so that they can't sneak in before the return throw. Use a run down play if they try to go back.

NOTE:

This is a good play to use when you have bases loaded, for either bunts, or a ground ball hit down the first base line.

Bases Loaded 3-2-3, 1-2-3, 5-2-3 First, Pitcher, or Third- to Catcher- Back to First Double Play (NO.46)

1) **First Baseman** fields a bunt or a hit down the first base line. Immediately fire the ball to the catcher at home plate for the force out. Then they immediately go back to the first for a return throw from the catcher. Or **Third Baseman** or **Pitcher** field the bunt and immediately throw to the catcher for the force out. 2) **Catcher** comes right out in front of the plate and faces the direction of the thrower. They take the throw touch the bag with their foot, pivot and turn, and gun a throw back to first base to get the batter. 3) **First**

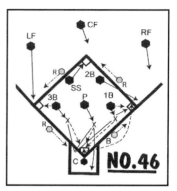

Baseman gets to first, touches the bag with their foot, stretches out and faces home for the return throw from the catcher for out number two.

NOTE:

This is a rare play, but it can result in a double play if your players and pitcher are observant at third base, and notice the runner has tagged up and left too soon on the fly ball catch.

Runner on Third 7-1-5, 8-1-5, 9-1-5 Outfielder- to Pitcher- to Third Double Play (NO.47)

1) **Outfielder** catches a fly ball for out number one. The ball is thrown back to the infield and gets to the pitcher. 2) Either the **Pitcher** or one of the infielders has noticed that the runner tagged up at third, but left too soon. The pitcher throws the

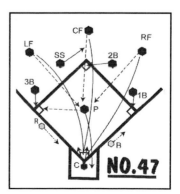

39

ball over to the third baseman. The pitcher or one of the infielders then appeals to the umpire. The umpire agrees because they also had noticed. 3) **Third Baseman** touches third base for out number two.

Triple Plays

Triple plays are very rare, especially in youth Baseball or Softball. Most of the time they start out at third base or shortstop. There has to be at least 2 runners on base and no outs. They usually start with a ground ball, but many times they start with either a soft or a hard line drive to an infielder, and then a tag out of a runner.

Runners on First and Second, or Bases Loaded 5-4-3 Third-to Second- to First Triple Play (NO.48)

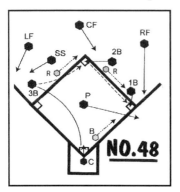

1) **Third Baseman** catches a line drive for out number one. They throw the ball to the second baseman covering. 2) **Second Baseman** tags the base or runner trying to get back to second for out two, then immediately fires the ball over to the first baseman covering. 3) **First Baseman** tags the base or the runner trying to get back to first base for out three.

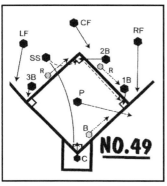

Runners on First and Second, or Bases Loaded 6-4-3 Short- to Second- to First Triple Play (NO.49)

1) **Shortstop** catches a line drive for out number one. They flip the ball to the second baseman covering. 2) **Second Baseman** tags the base or runner trying to get back to second for out two, then immediately fires the ball over to the first baseman covering. 3) **First Baseman** tags the base or the runner trying to get back to first base for out three.

NOTE:
Here is one that could work down at the lower levels or divisions. You have your outfield pulled in for a weak hitter, and they hit a line drive to one your corner outfielders. The runners start to go, but then don't get back to the base on time.

Bases Loaded 7-4-5, 9-6-3 Outfielder- to Second- to Third or First Triple Play (NO.50)
1) **Left or Right Fielder** catches a line drive for out number one. They immediately throw to second base. 2) Either the **Shortstop or Second Baseman** tags the base or the runner for out number two. They immediately fire the ball down to either third or first base. 3) **Third or First Baseman** tags the base or runner out number three.

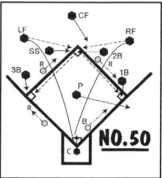

Outfielders Playing Shallow

Shallow outfield play is a lost art in most little league games. This is probably because most little league managers are afraid the ball will get by them. This is why you should have signals to position them, side to side, in or out. In most lower levels or divisions though the batters don't hit the ball that hard.

So you can determine good and weak hitters. Bring your outfielders in on the weak hitters. Also my advice is start a note book on the teams you may play again. The little kids need every advantage you can give them. And also when you have them playing shallow they are more into the game.

Runner on Third, or Bases Loaded Shallow Outfielder- to Home Plate Play (NO.51)
1) **Outfielders** are playing in. Ground ball is hit to them. They field the ball and make a one bounce throw to the catcher.
2) **Catcher** can see the hit is going right to the pulled in outfielder.

41

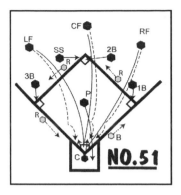

NO.51

So have them come right out in front of the plate and face the direction the throw is coming from. The one bounce throw should get to them lower so that they can swing around quicker to either touch the plate for the force out, or tag the runner sliding in.

Teach your catcher to know their outfielders. If the thrower has a strong arm and always throws the ball on a line to them, they can almost stand on the plate for a target when the force out is the play. If it's a tag the runner situation you can have them block the plate as long as they will have the ball.

Decoy Plays

"*Decoy*" plays sometimes help level the playing field when the other team is better than yours. These are plays where if you are not paying close attention, what you see is not really what happened or is going to happen. The player doing the decoying makes some kind of a move that makes everyone else think they are going to make a certain kind of throw or catch, then they actually do something else. Sort of like the Magicians slight of hand.

Outfield Plays
Ball is Hit over the Head of the Outfielder Play (NO.52)
1) **Outfielder** should learn to tell almost at the crack of the bat that

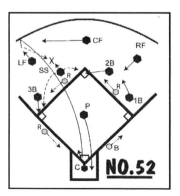

NO.52

the ball is going over their head. Knowing there are runners on base and there is a fence behind them, here is what they should do. They count to 4 seconds by "1000's". They keep looking at the ball as it starts to go over their head, then they put both hands up as if the catch the fly ball.

Then they pretend to make the catch. Then all of a sudden they whirl around, look for the ball bouncing back to them off the fence. 2) At least some of the runners will stay on the base to tag up on the fly ball because they think your are going to catch it. And that may delay their running around for extra bases. And it may save a run from scoring. I'm not suggesting the little kids do this, but maybe 12 or 13 and up. 3) For the real kids you will probably need to have your **Shortstop** go out and become the relay player. Unless the runner or batter is going to third, they turn and fire the ball to second base covering. When their back is to the plate have your catcher be the one to tell the relay player which base to turn and throw to.

NOTE:

For this to work though you have to have a wall or fence in the outfield, and the play will have to practiced a lot to get the timing and acting down.

Infield Plays

Runner on Second, or First and Second, Shortstop and Second Base Decoy Play (NO.53)

1) **Shortstop or Second Baseman** cheat in a little towards second base to keep runner in scoring position from getting too big of lead off. Then they take turns pretending to sneak over to the bag for a pick-off. If they act this out correctly, and the runner buys into it, this usually keeps the runner closer to the base. If the runner pays no attention to it and dares your pitcher to pick them off, then make the signal and run your second base pick-off play. 2) The pitcher can help the

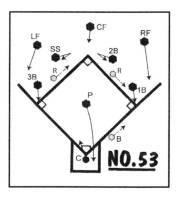

decoy, fake out the runner, work by stepping back off the rubber once in awhile, then faking a throw to second base.

Runner on First and Third, First Baseman Decoy Play (NO.54)

1) **First Baseman** plays right behind the runner and does not hold them on base. The runner will usually take a longer lead off then, thinking they can get an edge going down to second (the decoy).

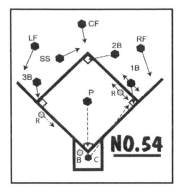

On a pre arranged signal with the catcher and pitcher, the first baseman breaks for the bag. 2) **Catcher** pops up after catching the pitch and guns a throw down to the first baseman to pick the runner off base. 3) Or the other decoy the **First Baseman** can use is the "shadow" technique. This is effective when the runner is over observant and always checking the first baseman as they take their lead.

How this works is the first baseman keeps lining up right behind them. As they move out farther or in closer, the first baseman stays directly behind them (shadowing). This will really make most runners very nervous, causing them to lose their focus on stealing second, or watching the batter for a hit.

While this play is taking place if there is a runner on third, make sure your first baseman watches them, and they do not sneak in to home plate to score.

Runner on First and Third, Catcher Decoy Play (NO.55)

1) **Catcher** watches the runner at first for acting like they want to steal second to get into scoring position. This all has to happen on a

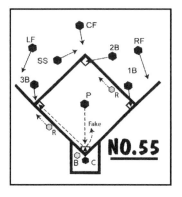

prearranged signal with the pitcher and third baseman.

This works best when there are already two outs, and the runner at third is taking a big lead off so that they can score and not get left stranded. The pitcher makes their pitch. 2) **Catcher** pops up after catching the pitch, fakes a throw down to second, then suddenly whirls around facing third and guns a throw down to third base. 3) **Third Baseman** breaks to third right as the catcher makes their pump fake down to second. Takes the throw and tags the runner trying to get back to third. This usually works because the runner hesitates thinking the catcher is going to throw down to second. In the worst case you trap the runner at third in a run down. If the runner on first does steal second, it's not going to make any difference because if the runner at third is picked off it is out number three.

Runner on First and Third, Pitcher Decoy Play (NO.56)

1) **Pitcher** watches the runner at first for acting like they want to steal second to get into scoring position. This all has to happen on a prearranged signal with the pitcher, third baseman, and first baseman.

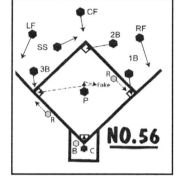

This probably works best when there are already two outs, and the runner at third is taking a big lead off so that they can score and not get left stranded. The pitcher gets up on the rubber and gets ready to make their pitch.

They go into their stretch position, wait for a few seconds then suddenly step back off the rubber, face first base and pump fake (the decoy) a pick-off throw to the first baseman. Following that they whirl all the way around and fire the ball over to the third baseman. 2) **Third Baseman** cheats a little closer to third. Then breaks for third just as the pitcher starts to step back off the rubber. They catch the throw and tag the runner out trying to get back to the base. Or they trap them into a run down and tag them out. This is a timing play so you will have to practice it a lot.

Hitting the Cutoff Plays

There is an advantage in using a cutoff player in youth Baseball or Softball. With the little kids they can't always throw too far or too accurate. Cutting the ball off before it gets to the plate has some advantages. Most throws from the outfield are weak anyway with little kids. So when the cutoff player cuts it off, they may trap a runner trying for an extra base.

Chances are rare that a throw from the outfield is going to get a runner at the plate anyway. The first baseman takes most cutoffs from right or center field. Third baseman takes most cutoffs from left field. I think a position between second base and the pitcher's mound is best for the little kids. Make sure your players know when you want them to use the cutoff and when not to. Teach your cutoff players to wave their arms so that the outfielder does not waste time trying to find them.

Several more suggestions. Designate your catcher to be the one tell the cutoff player where to throw to, or let the ball go through. Their instructions should be simple like say nothing (to let it go through to home plate), say, "Cut-Cut" (to cut off the ball and hold it). And say, "Cut and Relay to (base)" (to cut off the ball and throw it to a specific base).

Runners on Base, Hit Direct to Right Field, Right Center Field, Cutoff Play (NO.57)

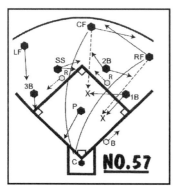

1) **First Baseman** moves to one of two infield cutoff positions depending on where the hit is located. 2) **Right or Center Fielder** fields the ball and throws towards home plate. 3) **Catcher** calls the play, cut it off or let it go. If they think they can get the runner at the plate they don't yell or say anything and the ball goes through to them. If they don't have a shot at the runner coming to the plate they may yell, "Cut and relay to third (or second)".

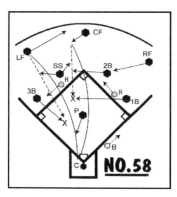

Runners on Base, Hit Direct to Left Field, Left Center Field, Cutoff Play (NO.58)

1) **First Baseman** moves to cutoff position behind the mound on hits to left center field. 2) **Third Baseman** moves to cutoff position about halfway to home plate on hits to left field 3) **Left or Center Fielder** fields the ball and throws towards home plate. 4) **Catcher** calls the

play, cut it off or let it go. If they think they can get the runner at the plate they don't yell or say anything and the ball goes through to them. If they don't have a shot at the runner coming to the plate they may yell something like, "Cut and relay to second".

Now to further complicate things they have "Double Cutoffs". These are for deep hits in the gap, or maybe when you have no outfield fence to stop the ball. Also it will probably be easier to teach when your kids are 12 years or older.

Bases Empty, Hit to Right Center Field Gap Deep, Double Cutoff Play (NO.59)

1) **First Baseman** checks that the batter touched first base, then trails them to second base. If the hit is fielded fairly quickly, then they cover second for the throw from the first or second cutoff.

2) **Second Baseman** goes way out on the grass and lines up with the player fielding the ball and third base, for the first cutoff. Unless otherwise instructed by the catcher, they take the first throw turn and throw to the shortstop trailing about 10 yards.

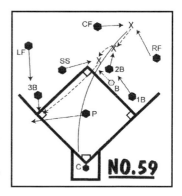

3) **Shortstop** goes out and trails the second baseman out on the edge of the infield, and lines up with third base as the second cutoff. Both the cutoff players need to be instructed by the catcher as to where to throw the ball as the play develops. You should probably come up with a coded call signal so that the runner does not know exactly what the cutoff players are going to do.

Bases Empty, Hit to Left Center Field Gap Deep, Double Cutoff Play (NO.60)

1) **First Baseman** checks that the batter touched first base, then trails them to second base. If the hit is fielded fairly quickly, then they cover second for the throw from the first or second cutoff.

2) **Shortstop** goes way out on the grass and lines up with the player fielding the ball and third base, for the second cutoff. Unless

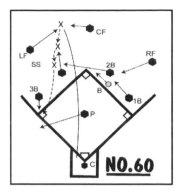

otherwise instructed by the catcher, they take the first throw, turn and throw to the second baseman trailing about 10 yards back for the second cutoff.

3) **Second Baseman** goes out and trails the shortstop out on the edge of the infield, and lines up with third base as the second cutoff. Both the cutoff players need to be instructed by the catcher as to where to throw the ball as the play develops. You should probably come up with a coded call signal so that the runner does not know exactly what the cutoff players are going to do.

Runner on First, Hit to Right Center Field Gap Deep, Double Cutoff Play (NO.61)

1) **First Baseman** moves to the second cutoff position on the edge of the infield grass and lined up with the player fielding the ball and home plate, for a second cutoff position to the plate.

2) **Second Baseman** goes way out on the outfield grass and lines

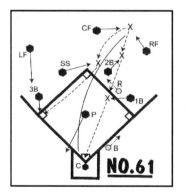

up with the player fielding the ball and home plate, for the first cutoff. Unless otherwise instructed by the catcher, they take the first throw turn and throw to the first baseman on the edge of the grass. 3) **Shortstop** goes out and trails the second baseman out on the edge of the infield, and lines up with third base and the outfielder fielding the ball as the second cutoff to third base. They repeat the call from the catcher to the second baseman on where to throw the ball.

Sometimes it's easier to get the batter at third base, than it is to get the lead runner at home plate. Both the cutoff players need to be instructed by the catcher as to where to throw the ball as the play develops. You should probably come up with a coded call signal so that the runner does not know exactly what the cutoff players are going to do.

Runner on First, Hit to Left Center Field Gap Deep, Double Cutoff Play (NO.62)

1) **First Baseman** moves to the second cutoff position on the edge of the infield grass and lined up with the player fielding the ball and home plate, for a second cutoff position to the plate. 2) **Shortstop** goes way out on the outfield grass and lines up with the player fielding the ball and home plate, for the first cutoff. Unless otherwise instructed by the catcher, they take the first throw turn and throw to the first baseman on the edge of the grass. 3) **Second Baseman** goes out and trails the second baseman out on the edge of the infield, and lines up with third base and the outfielder fielding the ball as the second cutoff to third

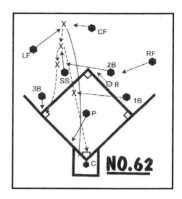

base. They repeat the call from the catcher to the shortstop on where to throw the ball.

Sometimes it's easier to get the batter at third base, than it is to get the lead runner at home plate. Both the cutoff players need to be instructed by the catcher as to where to throw the ball as the play develops. You should probably come up with a coded call signal so that the runner does not know what the cutoff players are doing.

Hitting the Relay Plays

There is an advantage in using a relay player in youth Baseball or Softball. With the little kids they can't always throw too far or too accurate. Relaying the ball in from the outfield instead of throwing all the way into the plate wildly has some advantages. Most throws from the outfield are weak anyway with little kids.

So most of the time they never even get to the plate. The throw to the relay player might trap a runner between bases. So these plays are really more important for the little beginner kids. Explain to your team that any time the ball is hit into the gap between outfielders, they need to have a relay player go out to relay the throw in. Have them wave their arms so that the outfielder can find them quickly without any trouble. This saves time.

Runners on Base, Hit to Left Center Field Gap, Relay Play (NO.63)

1) **Shortstop** moves to a relay position out in the grass behind the second base. The weaker the throw from the outfielder fielding the

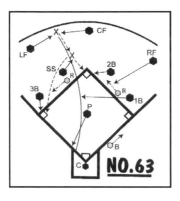

ball, the closer they have to get to the outfielder. If there is an outfield fence, they need to be about half the distance between the ball and second base, then go from there. 2) **Second Baseman** moves to cover second base. 3) Third **Baseman** covers third base. The best chance to get the runner will probably be at third or home. 4) **Left or Center Fielder** fields the ball and throws immediately to the shortstop (relay player). 5) **First Baseman** trails the runner as they move to second base. 6) **Catcher** calls where the shortstop should throw, "Second Base", "Third Base", or "Home". If the runners or batter are already home they can just say, "Throw to pitcher".

Runners on Base, Hit Down Left Field Line In the Corner, Relay Play (NO.64)

1) **Shortstop** moves to a relay position out in the grass near the left field line. The weaker the throw from the outfielder fielding the ball, the closer they have to get to the outfielder. If there is an outfield fence, they need to be about half the distance between the ball and

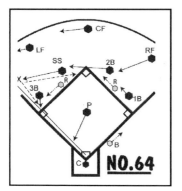

third base, then go from there. 2) **Second Baseman** trails the shortstop and moves to a position on the edge of the grass, in line with the ball and second base. 3) Third **Baseman** covers third base. The best chance to get the runner will probably be at third or home. 4) **Left Fielder** fields the ball and throws immediately to the shortstop (relay player). 5) **First Baseman** trails the runner as they move to second base. 6) **Catcher** calls where the shortstop should throw, "Second Base", "Third Base", or "Home". If the runners or batter are already home they can just say, "Throw to pitcher".

Runners on Base, Hit to Right Center Field Gap, Relay Play (NO.65)

1) **Second Baseman** moves to a relay position out in the grass behind the second base, and in line with third base . The weaker the throw from the outfielder fielding the ball, the closer they have to get. If there is an outfield fence, they need to be about half the distance between the ball and second base, then go from there. 2) **Shortstop** trails second baseman and moves to cover second base. 3) Third **Baseman** covers third base. The best chance to get the runner will probably be at third or home. 4) **Right or Center Fielder** fields the ball and throws immediately

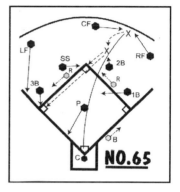

to the second baseman (relay player). 5) **First Baseman** moves to a cutoff position in case there is a weak throw to home. 6) **Catcher** calls where the second baseman should throw, "Second Base", "Third Base", or "Home". If the runners and batter are already home they can just say, "Throw to pitcher".

Runners on Base, Hit Down Right Field Line In the Corner, Relay Play (NO.66)

1) **Second Baseman** moves to a relay position out in the grass near the right field line. The weaker the throw from the outfielder fielding the ball, the closer they have to get to the outfielder. If there is an outfield fence, they need to be about half the distance between the ball and first base, then go from there. 2) **Shortstop** trails the second baseman

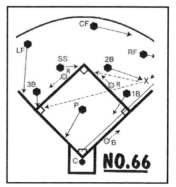

51

and moves to a position to cover second base. 3) Third **Baseman** covers third base. The best chance to get the runner will probably be at third or home. 4) **Right Fielder** fields the ball and throws immediately to the second baseman (relay player). 5) **First Baseman** takes a cutoff position in case there is a throw to the plate. 6) **Catcher** calls where the second baseman should throw, "Second Base", "Third Base", or "Home". If the batter is already home they can just say, "Throw to pitcher".

Different Situation Plays

These are the ways you handle the hits and where you go out in the field for each different situation. Basically we will show the situation you will most likely encounter in almost every game. There are other variations of these plays and strategies that the professionals use. If your team can learn just these plays they will do fine in baseball. Explain to your players that they need to learn to know who is at bat, how many outs there are, and where the runners on base are at, just before every play starts. Next they should ask themselves, "what will I do if the ball comes to me". Then be ready if it does.

Bases Empty, Single to left, Play (NO.67)

1) **Left Fielder** fields the ball. If it's a short single, they throw to second base ahead of the runner. If it's a long single, they throw to

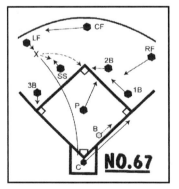

the relay player (shortstop). 2) **First Baseman** checks to see if the batter touches first base. Then they move over and back up any throws to second base. 3) **Second Baseman** moves over to cover second base for a throw. 4) **Shortstop** chases out after the ball. Then they line up between the left fielder and second base, in case a relay throw is needed. 5) **Third Baseman** covers third base.

6) **Center Fielder** runs over to back up the left fielder. 7) **Right Fielder** moves into position in a line between the left fielder and second base, just in case there is an over throw. 8) **Pitcher** moves

towards second base to help back up any throws. 9) **Catcher** covers first in case the runner takes too wide a turn.

Bases Empty, Single to Center, Play (NO.68)

1) **Center Fielder** fields the ball. If it's a short single, they throw to second base ahead of the runner. If it's a long single, they throw to the relay player (shortstop).

2) **First Baseman** checks to see if the batter touches first base. Then they move over and cover first on the inside. 3) **Second Baseman** moves over to cover second base for a throw. 4) **Shortstop** chases out after the ball. Then they line up between the center fielder and second base, in case a relay throw is needed. 5) **Third Baseman** covers

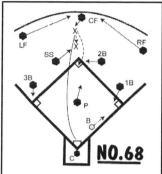

third base. 6) **Left and Right Fielders** run over to back up the left fielder. 7) **Pitcher** moves to just behind the mound to help back up any throws to second. 8) **Catcher** covers home in case the runner comes around and tries to come home.

Bases Empty, Single to Right Play (NO.69)

1) **Right Fielder** fields the ball. If it's a short single, they throw to second base ahead of the runner. If it's a long single, they may want to throw to the relay player (second baseman). 2) **First Baseman** checks to see if the batter touches first base. Then they move over and cover first on the inside. 3) **Second Baseman** chases out after the ball. Then they line up between the right fielder and second base, in case a relay throw is needed. 4) **Shortstop** moves over to cover second base for a throw. 5) **Third**

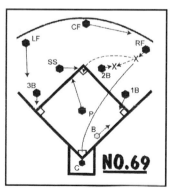

Baseman covers third base. 6) **Center Fielder** runs over to back up the right fielder.

7) **Left Fielder** moves towards the infield to back up any over throws to second base. 8) **Pitcher** follows the flight of the ball, then decides whether to help back up throws to either second or first. 9) **Catcher** covers home in case the runner comes around and tries to come home.

Bases Empty, Double or Triple to Left Center Field Gap, Play NO.70) See Play NO.60 Diagram
1) **Center Fielder** fields the ball. They throw to the relay player (shortstop). 2) **First Baseman** checks to see if the batter touches first base. Then they trail the batter to second, and stay there to cover the base for any throws. 3) **Second Baseman** trails the shortstop to the second cutoff position behind them, and in line between the center fielder and third base. 4) **Shortstop** moves way out on the grass as the first cutoff. Then lines up between the center fielder and third base. They can throw to the second cutoff or third. Catcher tells them where to throw. 5) **Third Baseman** covers third base. 6) **Left Fielder** runs over to back up the center fielder. 7) **Right Fielder** moves in towards the infield to back up any possible over throws to second base. 8) **Pitcher** moves over and backs up throw to third. 9) **Catcher** covers home in case the runner comes around and tries to come home. Also yells to the cutoff or relay players where to throw the ball.

Bases Empty, Double or Triple Down the Left Field Line, Play NO.71) See Play NO.64 Diagram
1) **Left Fielder** fields the ball. They throw to the relay player (shortstop). 2) **First Baseman** checks to see if the batter touches first base. Then they trail the batter to second, and stay there to cover the base for any throws. 3) **Second Baseman** trails the shortstop to the second cutoff position behind them, and in line between the left fielder and second base. 4) **Shortstop** moves way out on the grass as the first cutoff. Then lines up between the left fielder and third base. They can throw to the second cutoff or third. Catcher tells them where to throw. 5) **Third Baseman** covers third base. 6) Center **Fielder** runs over to back up the left fielder. 7) **Right Fielder** moves in towards the infield to back up any over throws to second base. 8) **Pitcher** moves over and backs up throw

to third. 9) **Catcher** covers home in case the runner comes around and tries to come home. Also yells to the cutoff or relay players where to throw the ball.

Bases Empty, Double or Triple to Right Center Field Gap, Play NO.72) See Play NO.59 Diagram

1) **Center Fielder** fields the ball. They throw to the relay player (second baseman). 2) **First Baseman** checks to see if the batter touches first base. Then they trail the batter to second, and stay there to cover the base for any throws. 3) **Shortstop** trails the second baseman to the second cutoff position behind them, and in line between the center fielder and second base. 4) **Second Baseman** moves way out on the grass as the first cutoff. Then lines up between the center fielder and third base. They can throw to the second cutoff or third. Catcher tells them where to throw. 5) **Third Baseman** covers third base. 6) **Left Fielder** moves to back up the third baseman. 7) **Right Fielder** runs to back up the center fielder 8) **Pitcher** moves over and backs up throw to third. 9) **Catcher** covers home in case the runner comes around and tries to come home. Also yells to the cutoff or relay players where to throw the ball.

Bases Empty, Double or Triple Down the Right Field Line, Play NO.73) Similar to Play NO.66 Diagram

1) **Right Fielder** fields the ball. They throw to the relay player (second baseman). 2) **First Baseman** checks to see if the batter touches first base. Then they trail the batter to second, and stay there to cover the base for any throws. 3) **Second Baseman** moves way out on the grass near the first base line as the first cutoff. Then lines up between the right fielder and third base. They can throw to the second cutoff or third. Catcher tells them where to throw. 4) **Shortstop** trails the second baseman to the second cutoff position behind them, but in line between the right fielder and home plate. 5) **Third Baseman** covers third base. 6) **Left Fielder** runs over to back up any throws to third base. 7) **Center Fielder** runs over to back up the right fielder. 8) **Pitcher** moves over and backs up throw to third, instead of up near home plate. 9) **Catcher** covers home in case the runner comes around and tries to come home. Also yells to the cutoff or relay players where to throw the ball.

Bases Empty, Pop Fly to Shallow Left Field, Play NO.74)

1) **Left Fielder** calls for the ball if they think they can make the play. All the other players have to yield to them. 2) **First Baseman** covers first base. 3) **Second Baseman** covers second base 4) **Shortstop** calls for the ball if they think they can make the play. Otherwise they give way if the left fielder has called for it. 5) **Third Baseman** calls for the ball if they think they can make the play. Otherwise they give way if the left fielder or the shortstop calls them off. 6) **Center Fielder** runs over to back up the left fielder. 7) **Right Fielder** moves over in line with second base and backs up any over throws. 8) **Pitcher** stands near mound and tells which infielder is closest to the ball if it is going to land in the infield. If not they cover third base. 9) **Catcher** backs up any throws to third base.

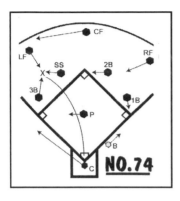

Bases Empty, Pop Fly to Shallow Center Field, Play NO.75)

1) **Center Fielder** calls for the ball if they think they can make the play. All the other players have to yield to them. 2) **First Baseman** covers first base unless both the second baseman and shortstop go for the ball. In that case they have to move over and cover second. 3) **Second Baseman** calls for the ball if they think they can make the play. Otherwise they give way if the center fielder or shortstop has called for it before they do. Whichever player is called off the ball, either the second baseman or the shortstop, has to cover second base. 4) **Shortstop** calls for the ball if they think they can make the play. Otherwise they give way if the center fielder or the second baseman has called for it before they do. 5) **Third Baseman** covers third base. 6) **Left Fielder**

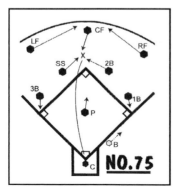

and Right Fielder run over to back up the center fielder.

7) **Pitcher** stands near mound and tells which infielder is closest to the ball if it is going to land in the infield. If not they cover second base when the first baseman is unable to get over to cover for the second baseman and shortstop because they both went out for the pop fly. 9) **Catcher** backs up any throws to third base.

Bases Empty, Pop Fly to Shallow Right Field, Play NO.76)

1) **Right Fielder** calls for the ball if they think they can make the play. All the other players have to yield to them. 2) **First Baseman** calls for the ball if they think they can make the play. Otherwise they give way if the right fielder or the second baseman calls them off. 3) **Second Baseman** calls for the ball if they think they can make the play. Otherwise they give way if the right fielder has called for it first. 4) **Shortstop** covers second base 5) **Third Baseman** covers third base. 6) **Center Fielder** runs over to back up the right fielder. 7) **Left Fielder** moves over behind third base and backs up any over throws. 8)

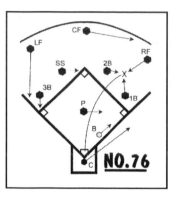

Pitcher stands near mound and tells which infielder is closest to the ball if it is going to land in the infield. If not they cover first base. 9) **Catcher** backs up any throws to first base.

Bases Empty, Bunt in Front of Plate, Play NO.77)

1) **Catcher** covers home plate. They have priority to get to all the balls out in front of the plate, and half way to the pitcher, if possible. Pitcher, first baseman, and third base yield to catcher unless it is a hard bunt right to them. 2) **First Baseman** charges the plate and covers the right side of the infield. Throws to second

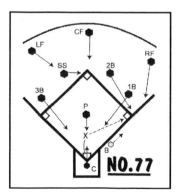

baseman covering first if they have to field the ball. 3) **Pitcher** covers the middle of the infield. Throws to first if they field the ball. 4) **Third Baseman** charges the plate and covers the left side of the infield. Throws to first if they field the ball. 5) **Second Baseman** moves over and covers first. 6) **Shortstop** covers second base. 7) **Left Fielder** moves towards the infield to back up any poor throws. 8) **Center Fielder** backs up any throws to second base. 9) **Right Fielder** backs up any throws to first base.

Runner on First or First and Third, Single to Left, Play (NO.78)
1) **Left Fielder** fields the ball. Throws to cutoff player (shortstop). If shortstop is out of position they throw to third base. 2) **First Baseman** checks to see if the batter touches first base.

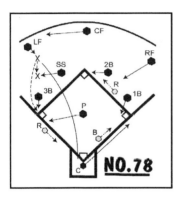

Then they cover first base on the infield side. 3) **Second Baseman** covers second base. 4) **Shortstop** chases out after the ball. Then they line up between the left fielder and third base as the cutoff player, in case a relay throw is needed. 5) **Third Baseman** covers third base, and backs up the shortstop. 6) **Center Fielder** runs over to back up the left fielder. 7) **Right Fielder** moves in towards the infield just in case there is a bad throw. 8) **Pitcher** follows the flight of the ball. Then they decide which base to back up. Usually it's third base. 9) **Catcher** moves over and backs up first.

Runner on First or First and Third, Single to Center, Play (NO.79)
1) **Center Fielder** fields the ball. Throws to cutoff player (shortstop). If shortstop is out of position they throw to third base. 2) **First Baseman** checks to see if the batter touches first base. Then they move over and cover first on the infield side. 3) **Second Baseman** moves over to cover second base for a throw. 4) **Shortstop** chases out after the ball. Then they line up between the center fielder and third base, in case a relay throw is needed. 5) **Third**

Baseman covers third base. 6) **Left and Right Fielders** both run over to back up the center fielder. 7) **Pitcher** moves to back up any throws to third. 8) **Catcher** covers home in case a runner comes around and tries to come home.

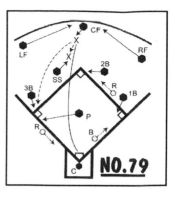

Runner on First or First and Third, Single to Right, Play (NO.80)
   1) **Right Fielder** fields the ball. Throws to the cutoff player (shortstop) 2) **First Baseman** checks to see if the batter touches first base. Then they move over and cover first on the inside. 3) **Second Baseman** covers second base. 4) **Shortstop** moves over to the cutoff position between right fielder and third base. 5) **Third Baseman** covers third base. 6) **Center Fielder** runs over to back up the right fielder. 7) **Left Fielder** moves towards the infield to back up throws to third base. 8) **Pitcher** moves to back up third base. 9) **Catcher** covers home in case a runner comes around and tries to come home.

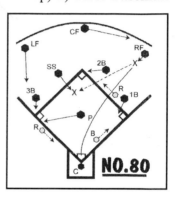

Runner on Second, First and Second, or Bases Loaded, Single to Left, Play (NO.81)
   1) **Left Fielder** fields the ball. Throws to cutoff player (third baseman) 2) **First Baseman** covers first base. 3) **Second Baseman** covers second base. 4) **Shortstop** covers third base. 5) **Third Baseman** moves to the cutoff position on the infield, and in line between the left fielder and home plate.

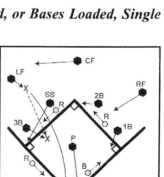

6) **Center Fielder** runs over to back up the left fielder. 7) **Right Fielder** moves in towards the infield, and backs up second base. 8) **Pitcher** moves in and backs up home plate. 9) **Catcher** covers home plate, and instructs the cutoff player (third baseman) where to throw.

Runner on Second, First and Second, or Bases Loaded, Single to Center, Play (NO.82)

1) **Center Fielder** fields the ball. Gets instruction from the left or right fielder on which cutoff to throw to, either third base

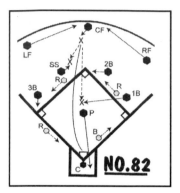

or home plate. 2) **First Baseman** moves to a position near the mound, and in line with the center fielder and home, to become the cutoff for home plate. 3) **Second Baseman** moves over to cover second base. 4) **Shortstop** moves to a cutoff position, lining up between the center fielder and third base. 5) **Third Baseman** covers third base. 6) **Left and Right Fielders** run over to back up the center fielder. Then they become quarterbacks and tell the center fielder where to throw. 7) **Pitcher** moves to back up any throws to home plate. 8) **Catcher** covers home in case a runner comes around and tries to score.

Runner on Second, First and Second, or Bases Loaded, Single to Right Play (NO.83)

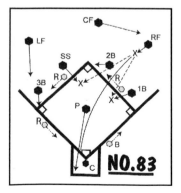

1) **Right Fielder** fields the ball. Gets instruction from the center fielder on which cutoff to throw to, either third base or home plate.
2) **First Baseman** moves to a position on the edge of the infield, and in line with the right fielder and home, to become the cutoff for home plate. 3) **Second Baseman** covers second base. 4) **Shortstop** moves towards

the infield, and in line between the right fielder and third base to become the cutoff for throws to third. 5) **Third Baseman** covers third base. 6) **Center Fielder** runs over to back up the right fielder. Then they become quarterbacks and tell the right fielder where to throw. 7) **Left Fielder** moves in towards third base so they can help back up at third or even second base. 8) **Pitcher** moves to a spot just behind the plate to back up home. Then they watch the play and back up any throws to home or third base. Usually it's home though. 9) **Catcher** covers home on throws, in case a runner comes around and tries to score.

Bases Empty, Double or Triple Down Left Field Line, Play (NO.84)

1) **Left Fielder** goes into the corner and fields the ball. Then they throw to the cutoff (shortstop) for the relay. 2) **First Baseman** checks to see if the batter touches first base. Then they trail the runner over to second, stop and cover second base. 3) **Second Baseman** trails the shortstop, stops out in front of the base, then stays near second. 4) **Shortstop** moves to a cutoff position down the left field line, lining up between the left fielder and third base. 5) **Third Baseman** covers third base. 6) **Center Fielder** runs over to back up the left fielder. 7) **Right Fielder** moves in and backs

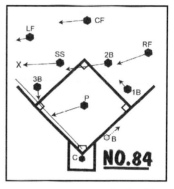

up second base on throws. 8) **Pitcher** moves over towards the line to back up any throws to third base. 9) **Catcher** covers home in case a runner comes around and tries to score.

Bases Empty, Double or Triple to Left Center Field Gap, Play (NO.85)

1) **Center Fielder** fields the ball. Then they throw to the cutoff (shortstop) for the relay. 2) **First Baseman** checks to see if the batter touches first base. Then they trail the runner over to second, stop and cover second base. 3) **Second Baseman** trails the shortstop, stops near the edge of the infield, then stays in line

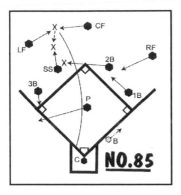

with home plate. 4) **Shortstop** moves to a cutoff position, then lines up between the center fielder and third base. 5) **Third Baseman** covers third base. 6) **Left Fielder** runs over to back up the center fielder. 7) **Right Fielder** moves in and backs up second base on throws. 8) **Pitcher** moves over towards the line to back up any throws to third base. 9) **Catcher** covers home in case the runner comes around and tries to score.

Bases Empty, Double or Triple to Right Center Field Gap, Play (NO.86)

1) **Center Fielder** fields the ball. Then they throw to the cutoff (second baseman) for the relay. 2) **First Baseman** checks

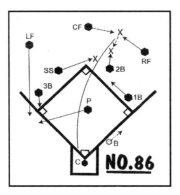

to see if the batter touches first base. Then they trail the runner over to second, stop and cover second base. 3) **Second Baseman** moves to a cutoff position out on grass, then lines up between the right fielder and third base. 4) **Shortstop** trails the second baseman, stops near second, then stays behind the base as a back up. 5) **Third Baseman** covers third base. 6) **Left Fielder** comes up to back up any throws to third base. 7) **Right Fielder** runs over and backs up the center fielder. 8) **Pitcher** moves over to back up third base. 9) **Catcher** covers home in case the runner comes around and tries to score.

Bases Empty, Double or Triple Down Right Field Line, Play (NO.87)

1) **Right Fielder** goes into the corner and fields the ball. Then they throw to the cutoff (second baseman) for the relay. 2) **First Baseman** checks to see if the batter touches first base. Then

62

they trail the runner over to second, stop and cover second base. 3) **Second Baseman** trails the shortstop, stops out in front of the base, then stays near second.

4) **Shortstop** moves to a back up position behind second base, lining up between the right fielder and second base. 5) **Third Baseman** covers third base. 6) **Center Fielder** runs over to back up the right fielder. 7) **Left Fielder** moves in towards third and backs up third base on throws. 8) **Pitcher** moves over towards the line to back up any throws to third base.

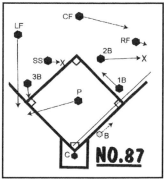

9) **Catcher** covers home in case a runner comes around and tries to score.

Runners on Base, Double or Triple Down Left Field Line, Play (NO.88)

1) **Left Fielder** goes into the corner and fields the ball. Then they throw to the cutoff (shortstop) for the relay. 2) **First Baseman** checks to see if the batter touches first base. Then they trail the runner over to second, stop and cover second base. 3) **Second Baseman** trails the shortstop, stops out in front of the base, then stays near second and lets the shortstop know where to throw. 4) **Shortstop** moves to a cutoff position down the left field line, lining up between the left fielder and third base. 5) **Third**

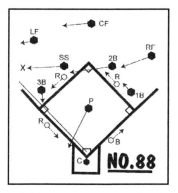

Baseman covers third base. 6) **Center Fielder** runs over to back up the left fielder. 7) **Right Fielder** moves in and backs up second base on throws. 8) **Pitcher** moves over towards the line and closer to home, and watches the play. Then backs up where the throw goes, either to third or home. 9) **Catcher** covers home in case a runner comes around and tries to score.

Runners on Base, Double or Triple to Left Center Field Gap, Play (NO.89)

1) **Center Fielder** fields the ball. Then they throw to the cutoff (shortstop) for the relay. 2) **First Baseman** takes the infield

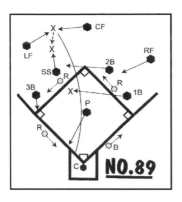

cutoff position between the left fielder and home plate. 3) **Second Baseman** trails the shortstop to a position behind them. Then lets them know where to throw. 4) **Shortstop** moves to a cutoff position, then lines up between the center fielder and home plate. 5) **Third Baseman** covers third base. 6) **Left Fielder** runs over to back up the center fielder. 7) **Right Fielder** moves in and backs up second base on throws. 8) **Pitcher** moves over towards the line and closer to home, and watches the play. Then backs up where the throw goes, either to third or home. 9) **Catcher** covers home in case a runner comes around and tries to score.

Runners on Base, Double or Triple to Right Center Field Gap, Play (NO.90)

1) **Center Fielder** fields the ball. Then they throw to the cutoff (second baseman) for the

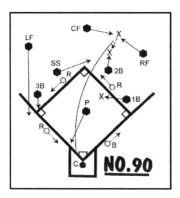

relay. 2) **First Baseman** takes an infield cutoff position on a line between the right fielder and the plate, for a throw to the plate.

3) **Second Baseman** moves to a cutoff position out on grass, then lines up between the right fielder home plate. 4) **Shortstop** trails the second baseman, stops near second, then lines up between the right fielder and third base. Then they tell the second baseman where to throw. 5) **Third Baseman** covers third base.

6) **Left Fielder** comes up to back up any throws to third base.

7) **Right Fielder** runs over and backs up the center fielder.

8) **Pitcher** moves over towards the line and closer to home, and watches the play. Then backs up where the throw goes, either to third or home. 9) **Catcher** covers home in case a runner comes around and tries to score.

Runners on Base, Double or Triple Down Right Field Line, Play (NO.91)

1) **Right Fielder** goes into the corner and fields the ball. Then they throw to the cutoff (second baseman) for the relay. 2) **First Baseman** takes an infield cutoff position on a line between the right fielder and the plate, for a throw to the plate. 3) **Second Baseman** moves to a cutoff position out on grass, then lines up between the right fielder home plate. 4) **Shortstop** moves to a cutoff position behind second base, lining up between the right fielder and third base. Then they tell the second baseman where to throw. 5) **Third Baseman** covers third base. 6) **Center Fielder** runs over to back up the right fielder. 7) **Left**

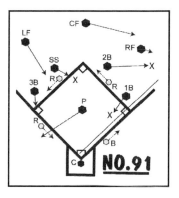

Fielder moves in towards the infield and backs up any throws to second or third base. 8) **Pitcher** moves way over on the other side of the base line halfway between third and home, watches the play evolve, then backs up the throw to either third or home. 9) **Catcher** covers home in case a runner comes around and tries to score.

Runner on First, Sacrifice Bunt in Front of Plate, Play (NO.92)

1) **Catcher** covers home plate. They have priority to get to all the balls right out in front of the plate, and half way to the pitcher if possible. Pitcher, first baseman, and third base yield to catcher unless it is a hard bunt right to them. Catcher tells the infielders where to throw. 2) **First**

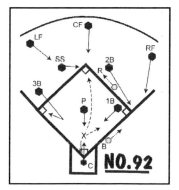

Baseman holds the runner on. Then charges the plate and covers the right side of the infield. If they field the ball, they listen for the catcher's instructions, then they throw to the appropriate base. 3) **Second Baseman** moves over and covers first. 4) **Pitcher** covers the middle of the infield. If they field the ball, they listen for the catcher's instructions, then they throw to the appropriate base. 5) **Third Baseman** charges the plate and covers the left side of the infield. If they field the ball, they listen for the catcher's instructions, then they throw to the appropriate base. If they don't field the ball, they quickly run back and cover third. 6) **Shortstop** covers second base. 7) **Left Fielder** moves towards the infield to back up any bad throws. 8) **Right Fielder** moves over behind first base and backs up over throws. 9) **Center Fielder** backs up throws to second base.

Runner on First and Second, Sacrifice Bunt is Towards Third Base, Defense Goes for the Out at First, Play (NO.93)

     1) **Catcher** covers home plate. They have priority to get to all the balls close to the plate, and half way to the pitcher if possible, then they throw to first. Pitcher, first baseman, and third base yield to catcher unless it is a hard bunt in their area. Catcher tells the infielders where to throw. 2) **First Baseman** charges the plate and covers the right side of the infield. If they field the ball, they listen

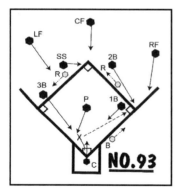

for the catcher's instructions, then they throw to the appropriate base. 3) **Second Baseman** moves over and covers first base. 4) **Pitcher** covers the third base line. If they field the ball, they listen for the catcher's instructions, then they throw to the appropriate base. 5) **Third Baseman** charges the plate and covers the left side of the infield. If they field the ball, they listen for the catcher's instructions, then they throw to the appropriate base. 6) **Shortstop** covers second base. 7) **Left Fielder** moves towards infield, then backs up throws to second or third. 8) **Right Fielder** moves over behind first base and backs up any over throws. 9) **Center Fielder** moves in and backs up any throws to second base.

Runner on First and Second, Sacrifice Bunt is Towards First Base, Defense Goes for Force Out at Third, Wheel Play (NO.94)

1) **Catcher** covers home plate. They have priority to get to all the balls close to the plate, and half way to the pitcher if possible, then they throw to third. Pitcher, first baseman, and third base yield to catcher unless it is a hard bunt in their area. Catcher tells the infielders where to throw. 2) **First Baseman** charges the plate and covers the right side of the infield. If they field the ball, they listen for the catcher's instructions, then they throw to the appropriate base. 3) **Second Baseman** moves over and covers first base. 4) **Pitcher** covers the middle of the infield. If they field the

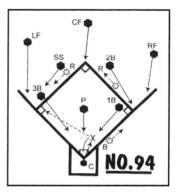

ball, they listen for the catcher's instructions, then they throw to the appropriate base. The shortstop is going to break for third just before they deliver their pitch. 5) **Third Baseman** charges the plate and covers the left side of the infield. If they field the ball, they listen for the catcher's instructions, then they throw to the appropriate base. 6) **Shortstop** get right behind the lead runner's right shoulder, then breaks for third just as the pitcher sets and starts to pitch. 7) **Left Fielder** moves towards third, then backs up throws there. 8) **Right Fielder** moves over behind first base and backs up any throws there. 9) **Center Fielder** moves in and covers second base.

Runner on First and Second, Pick-off at Second, Defense Goes for Fake Wheel Play Wheel Play (NO.95)

1) **Catcher** covers home plate. 2) **First Baseman** charges and covers the right side of the infield. Just like the wheel play is on. 3) **Pitcher** makes their pick-off throw to second just as the shortstop breaks for third. 4) **Third Baseman** charges

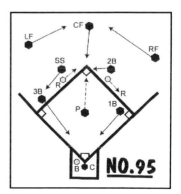

and covers the left side of the infield just like when the wheel play is on. 5) **Shortstop** get right behind the lead runner's right shoulder, then breaks for third just like the wheel play is on. 6) **Left Fielder** runs and backs up center field. 7) **Right Fielder** runs and backs up center field. 8) **Center Fielder** moves in and backs up the pick-off throw to second. 9) **Second Baseman** fakes a step towards first, then turns around and breaks for the pick-off at second, just as the shortstop breaks for third.

Runners on Base, Pop Fly to Shallow Left Field, Play (NO.96)

1) **Left Fielder** calls for the ball if they think they can make the play. All the other players have to yield to them. 2) **First Baseman** covers first base. 3) **Second Baseman** covers second

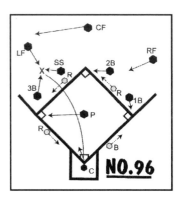

base 4) **Shortstop** calls for the ball if they think they can make the play. Otherwise they give way if the left fielder has called for it. 5) **Third Baseman** calls for the ball if they think they can make the play. Otherwise they give way if the left fielder or the shortstop calls them off. 6) **Center Fielder** runs over to back up left field. 7) **Right Fielder** moves over in line with second base and backs up any over throws. 8) **Pitcher** stands near mound and tells which infielder is closest to the ball if it is going to land in the infield. If not they cover third base. 9) **Catcher** covers home plate.

Runners on Base, Pop Fly to Shallow Center Field, Play (NO.97)

1) **Center Fielder** calls for the ball if they think they can make the play. All the other players have to yield to them. 2) **First Baseman** covers first base unless both the second baseman and shortstop go for the ball. In that case they have to move over and cover second. 3) **Second Baseman** calls for the ball if they think they can make the play. Otherwise they give way if the center fielder or shortstop has called for it before they do. Whichever player

is called off the ball, either the second baseman or the shortstop, has to cover second base. 4) **Shortstop** calls for the ball if they think they can make the play. Otherwise they give way if the center fielder or the second baseman has called for it before they do. 5) **Third Baseman** covers third base. 6) **Left Fielder & Right Fielder** run over to back up center field.

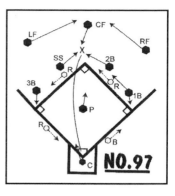

7) **Pitcher** stands near mound and calls which infielder is closest to the ball if it is going to land in the infield. If not they cover second base when the first baseman is unable to get there to cover. 8) **Catcher** covers home plate.

Runners on Base, Pop Fly to Shallow Right Field, Play (NO.98)

1) **Right Fielder** calls for the ball if they think they can make the play. All the other players have to yield to them. 2) **First Baseman** calls for the ball if they think they can make the play.

Otherwise they give way if the right fielder or the second baseman calls them off. 3) **Second Baseman** calls for the ball if they think they can make the play. Otherwise they give way if the right fielder has called for it first. 4) **Shortstop** covers second base 5) **Third Baseman** covers third base. 6) **Center Fielder** runs over to back up right field. 7) **Left Fielder** moves over behind third base and backs up

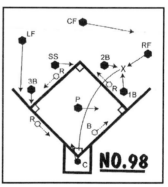

any throws there. 8) **Pitcher** stands near mound and tells which infielder is closest to the ball if it is going to land in the infield. If not they cover first base. 9) **Catcher** covers home plate.

Runners on Base, Pop Fly on the Infield, Play (NO.99)
Remember Though the Infield Fly Rule Applies.

1) **Pitcher** stands near the mound and calls the infielder who is closest to the ball to make the catch. If the catcher has to go

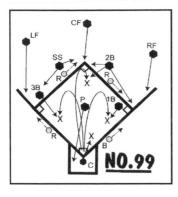

up the first or third base line to catch the pop fly, they have to cover home plate. 2) **First Baseman** covers their base if the pop fly is not to them. 3) **Second Baseman** covers their base if the pop fly is not to them. If the first baseman has to come in for the pop fly, they swing over and cover first. 4) **Shortstop** covers second base if the pop fly is not to them, and the second baseman is covering first or has to come in for the pop fly. If the third baseman has to come in for the pop fly, and the second baseman is covering second, then they cover third base. 5) **Third Baseman** covers third base if the pop fly is not to them. 6) **Center Fielder** comes in to back up second base. 7) **Left Fielder** comes in to back up third base. 8) **Right Fielder** comes in and backs up first base. 9) **Catcher** covers home plate unless they have to go out for the pop fly.

NOTE:

Why is this play important. Young youth players can very easily drop pop fly balls. And even though the batter is out, runners can advance at their own risk. So if an infielder is fumbling around with a dropped ball, and not paying attention, a runner on third could tag up and score. So make sure all your players pay close attention and stay alert for on this play.

Infield Drills

These are basically core training drills to help improve the play of your infielders. Pitchers can take part in some of these drills also. The more you do these the better their muscle memory gets.

Around the Horn, Drill (NO.100)

Actually this is more like a game than a drill. But they are learning without even knowing it. Works great for little beginning kids. It teaches them to toe touch the base, and make quick throws to another base. This helps them with their fielding ground balls and making double plays.

How this works is you get all your infielders including the pitcher out on the infield just like you are going to take a pregame infield practice. You say, "Get One" (1 out at first) and hit a ground ball to your first baseman. They field it, take it to the bag, touch it with a foot, and throws it down to the shortstop covering second. They get the throw, touch the bag with their foot, and throw it down to the third baseman covering third. They get the throw, touch the bag with their foot, and throw it down to

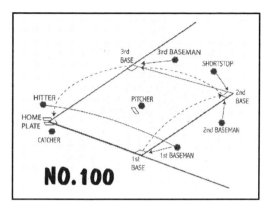

NO.100

the catcher at home plate. They touch home plate with their foot, and flip the ball to you or your coach to make the next hit.

Next you say, "Get One" and you hit a ground ball to the second baseman. They throw over to the first baseman , they take it to the bag, touch it with their foot, then throw it over to the shortstop covering second. They touch the bag with their foot, and throw it on around the horn back to home plate. This goes on until you have hit a grounder to all the infielders (including pitcher) and the catcher. What you do with the catcher is either flip the ball out in front of the plate or soft bunt it, say "Get One" and they field the ball and gun it down to first. Then it goes all the way around the horn and back to them.

The next time through you say, "Get Two" (a double play) and the ball gets thrown to whoever is covering second for one out (getting the lead runner). They field it, touch the bag, throw it back to first. First Baseman touches the bag, throws it back to second, and it goes around the horn back to home.

You keep doing this until you get through all the different types of outs you want them to get. You can do variations like go backwards around the horn (third-second-first-home). You will see that the more you do this the better their fielding gets. Also this is a great infield warm up before a game to psych out the opposition. I know it's probably not fair when your opponent is a team of real little kids, but it does tend to level the playing field a bit when you are outclassed sometimes by a hand picked team.

Shortstop/Second Baseman Reaction, Drill (NO.101)

This is a drill that really helps to make your shortstops and

NO.101

second baseman better at fielding the ball. Have your shortstops and second baseman all get in a group for this drill. One by one have them get into the fielding ready stance, preferably out at the shortstop position on a baseball field. Then what you do is stand up in front of home plate and hit, or throw, ground balls to them. For the real little kids I would throw the ball at first, then change to hitting with a bat as they get bigger.

Here is what you do. First hit it right at them, have them get their glove right down on the ground, field the ball and throw it back to you. Then as you progress you hit it farther and farther away from them to each side. They have to dive out sideways and catch or knock the ball down. When they have caught or knocked the ball down, they have to hold on to it, quickly get up, come under control and throw the ball back to you. After 2 tries each, rotate the players. I would run this drill fast for about 15 or 20 minutes, then go to something else. You should probably have at least 2 shortstops and 2 second basemen working on this drill every practice.

Infield Pop Fly Catching, Drill (NO.102)

This is a drill that really helps to make your infielders better at catching pop fly balls. Have your infielders all get in a group for this drill. Have them all get into their normal positions out on the infield. Then have your pitcher stand in front of the mound to direct traffic. This should help them not run into each other trying to catch the ball. Then one by one throw the ball way up in the air to each one. The pitcher watches the ball, determines which infielder is going to be closest to the ball, then yells out their position, "Third Base", "Second Base" etc. Make sure you show them first how to catch the ball using two hands. Throw at least 2 flies to each player as you move around the infield. Also don't forget to throw some up out in front of the plate for the catcher. Your pitcher gets out of the way and lets the infielders catch the fly balls, they just direct traffic. Work this drill 20 to 30 minutes each practice then move on to another drill.

NO.102

Stance Breakdowns, Drill (NO.103)

This is a drill that really helps to make your infielders better at relaxing then snapping into a ready position when play starts. Have your infielders all get in a group for this drill. Have them all go out into their normal positions out on the infield. Then you yell out,

A   **NO.103**   B

"Breakdown", and they snap down into their ready position for fielding *(SEE 103-A)*. Then you yell, "Pitch" and they all get their glove ready *(SEE 103-B)*. I would yell this about 5 times so that they all get to work on this at the same time. Then move on to another drill.

Tagging Runners, Drill (NO.104)

This is a drill that really helps to make your infielders better at tagging runners out as they come into a base, either standing up or sliding. Have your infielders all get in a group for this. Your third baseman, shortstop, and second baseman can do this at second base. Your first baseman can do this at first base. While you are

NO.104

running this drill have the other participating players stand back and watch. Instead of goofing around. Or if you have another coach, you can split into two groups and rotate.

You will need to have a runner for this drill. The runner can come in sliding some of the time, and standing up some of the time. Have your third baseman, shortstop, and second baseman each work on straddling the bag in front making a tag 2 times, then standing to the side sweeping a tag 2 times, then rotate. Then go to first base and work with your first baseman 2 times each way. You can also work on making the force out foot tag then getting out of the way to the side, or up in the air 2 times each. Work on this drill for about 45 minutes then move on to another drill.

NO.105

Infielders Throwing, Drill (NO.105)

This is a drill that really helps your infielders get better with their short snap throwing. First line them up facing each other in a row at about 10 to 15 yards between each other, then spaced apart about 4 or 5 yards Then they get down on one knee. Right knee if they are right handed, left knee if they are left handed.

74

Then have them throw back and forth to each other for about 15 or 20 minutes. After that move on to another drill. Try to run this drill each practice if possible, or every other practice. NOT just once.

Outfield Drills

These are basically core training drills to help improve the play of your outfielders. The more you do these the better their muscle memory gets.

Circling, Catching, and Relaying Fly Balls, Drill (NO.106)

This is a drill that really helps your outfielders get better at catching long high fly balls, and getting rid of them quickly to a relay player. Have all your outfielders line up in rows about 10 yards between each throwing partner, and about 5 yards apart in the row. They can spread out a little farther as they get bigger or better at this. Use one ball per each pair. First player throws the ball to their partner about a medium high fly ball. High enough though that they have time to circle around and get under it. The minute their partner throws the ball, they have to determine quickly about where it will land. Then they turn back toward the side the ball is on, then either go back a little and make a small circle or use drop step back with quick steps so that they are coming into the ball as they catch it.

They need to be half way through their little crow hop step in the air, ending up with their throwing hand side foot forward, just a seconds before they catch the ball. Then they throw it back to their partner sharply as they come down with the other foot while moving forward, just like they would to a relay or cutoff player. After each player has made 3 catches, the switch and let the thrower become the catcher. You can have them do this drill for about 15 to 20 minutes, then move on to another drill. If you can teach your outfielders to do this automatically, you will find that most teams won't run on you when the ball goes into your outfield.

Fielding Ground Balls and Relaying, Drill (NO.107)

This is a drill that really helps your outfielders get better at catching ground balls, then getting rid of them quickly to a relay

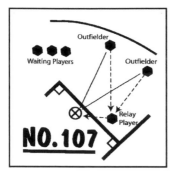

player. Have all your outfielders line up in two lines out in the outfield, maybe about 10-15 yards apart. You will need a relay player to catch the relay throws and flip them over to you.

Then you stand on the infield and hit or throw (for the little kids) the ball on the ground to them, first to one line then the other. They have to get in front of the ball, then down on one knee to block and catch the ball. After 3 grounders to each player rotate in 2 new players. Depending on how many outfielders you have, you can run this drill about 30 minutes. Then go to another drill.

Cutoff and Relay Throwing, Drill (NO.108)

This is a drill that really helps your outfielders get better at getting rid of the ball quickly to a relay or cutoff player. This sometimes referred to in baseball as the "Monkey in the Middle"

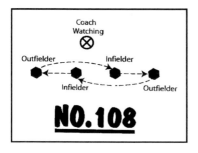

drill. First you get 4 outfielders lined up in a row. They can be about 15 yards between players for the little kids, and go up in distance from there depending on their age. The 2 middle players are infielders (relay & cutoff), and the 2 outside players are outfielders.

One of the infielders start the drill by throwing either a ground ball or fly ball to the outfielder on their side. As the outfielder catches the ball, the infielder that threw them the ball becomes a cutoff. The outfielder throws through that player on a bounce to the infielder on the other side of them (the relay). Then that infielder throws to the outfielder on their side and the play keeps going continuously until you or your coach says, "Stop".

Every once in awhile the coach can yell, "Cut", to make sure the outfielder is throwing a ball that can be cut off. Than have the cutoff player catch the ball cutting it off. Then they throw it to the other infielder player, and the drill starts over and keeps going. Rotate and switch players after 5 or 10 minutes or so. You can run this drill for about 20 or 30 minutes. Then move on to another drill. This way the players don't get too bored as they sometimes do. Make sure your outfielders are getting into the correct position as they are catching the ball.

Throwing to Home Plate, Drill (NO.109)

This is a drill that really helps your outfielders get better at getting rid of the ball quickly and making a throw to the plate. The real little kids are probably not going to be able to do this drill, but the older kids can. What your outfielders need to do is make a one or two bounce throw in line with the catcher out in front of the plate.

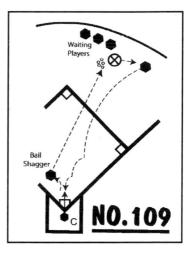

Then the catcher flips the ball to the shagger, who throws a roller back in the area of the you or your coach. The ball is lobbed up in the air by the coach to the outfielder, who has to get behind it and make a power throw in order to get it to the plate.

Show them how to make over hand throws by putting their two fingers on top of the ball, which puts back spin on the ball. They can check their throws to see if the bounces right or left it hits the ground. This means they are not putting the proper back spin over the top on the ball. After 3 throws rotate the thrower. Run this drill about 20 minutes depending on how many outfielders you have.

Catch on the Run, Drill (NO.110)

This is a drill that really helps your outfielders get better at catching the ball at a full run sprint. The real little kids are probably

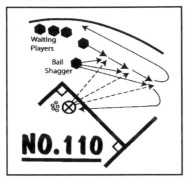

Waiting Players

Ball Shagger

NO.110

not going to be able to do this drill too well, but you can work with them to get better. How this works is you go out to the baseball field or park with lots of room. Have your outfielders form a line out about 40 or 50 feet in front of you, and about 30 feet to the side, either to the right or left. You or your coach will have 3 balls in your hands for this drill, and a bucket of balls ready to go.

The first outfielder, on your signal, "GO", sprints out straight ahead and parallel to you. You try to lead them like a QB throwing to receivers. You throw them the first ball (1). They have to try and catch it on a full run if possible. As they catch it they just drop it and keep running. Then they look for the next ball and react to it. Right after they drop the first ball, you then throw the next ball (2). Then throw the last ball (3), after they catch the second one.

After each ball have the shagger go out, pick it up, wait for the next, and after the third bring them all back to you. The player sprints back to the end of the line. Then you start all over again with 3 balls to the next player. Run this drill so that all your players get a chance to do it 3 times. Then call them all together and tell them you are going to challenge them. When you throw the third ball, you are going to throw it farther out ahead of them so that they have to dive for it to make the catch. What usually happen then is the kids forget they are tired and try to make a great play. Do the drill this way about 3 times at a practice session, for each outfielder.

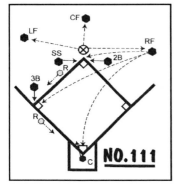

CF
LF
RF
SS
2B
R
3B
R
NO.111
C

Pick a Base, Drill (NO.111)

This is a drill that really helps your outfielders get better at catching the ball then throwing to the right base. The real little kids will need a lot a practice at this drill to get it right. What this teaches them is to get the proper step forward as they catch the ball, then learn the correct way to throw it. Go out to the baseball field, and put runners at second and third base. Then put a catcher, third baseman, shortstop, and second baseman at their regular positions to field the throws. Then have all your outfielders go out to there regular positions, except at shallow depth for the real little kids.

Then you or your coach stand just behind second base, and throw fly balls in all directions in the outfield. Just before you throw the ball though yell out what the situation is and where the throws should go. Make sure each one of your outfielders attempt to drop back, circle, or get behind the ball, then throw to the correct base. If they throw right handed they should have the right foot forward when they make the catch. And their left foot forward as they make the catch if they are left handed.

Have one of your coaches stand out in the center of the outfield and observe. If one of the players makes a mistake, have them pull that player aside, substitute another player for them to keep the drill going, then explain what they did wrong. Run this drill until every player gets at least 3 chances, then move on to another drill.

Hard Ball Pitching Drills

These are basically core training drills to help them improve on their pitching abilities. Make sure their arms are warmed up properly before engaging in any of these drills. They could do jumping jacks for a few minutes, or partner long toss back and forth for about 10 minutes at about 10 to 20 yards apart. I forgot to do this once when I was a teen ager, and my arm went totally dead (could not throw hard) on me for months.

Balanced Throwing, Drill (NO.112)

This is a neat little drill that might really help your pitchers keep their balance throughout their pitching motion, especially the little beginning pitchers. Doing this helps them learn to keep their weight back, keep their balance throughout their motion, and it lets their arm not fall behind the rest of their motion. You will need a 4 x 4 piece of wood about 6 to 7 feet long for this drill, depending on the size and age of the pitcher. Take it out to the grass. This way if they fall it won't be as hard as concrete, asphalt, or hard dirt.

What you have them do is stand near the middle of the 4 x 4, and have them go through windups and set (stretch) positions only. While lifting up their leg they have to stay balanced, go through the motion and stride out, and land the front foot on the 4 x 4 without falling off. It's kind of like a gymnast on a "balance beam".

Set Position

Wind Up Position
NO.112

Have each of your pitchers do each move 2 times then rotate pitchers. Depending on how many pitchers you have, I would have each one do the drill twice, then move on to another drill. The trick is do this every practice to build their muscle memory. Tell your pitchers to wear tennis shoes only on the days you do this drill..

Ball Delivery Slap, Drill (NO.113)
This is a drill to help develop their wrist snap, delivery of the ball out in front of their body, follow through, and defensive position after the delivery. To set this drill up you will need to cut up an old bed sheet. Cut it into pieces 18 inches long by 5 inches wide. Fold the long side so that each one is approximately 1 inch by 18 inches long. Form 2 lines facing each other, and spaced far enough apart so that the player using the wind up motion has their hand just missing their partners glove as they come down with their delivery.

The player in one line is down on one knee, with their glove side elbow resting on the up knee (probably the left). The arm on the up knee has the arm straight out

NO.113

parallel with the ground, glove on, palm up. The other line is standing up. That player holds out their throwing hand, palm up. The they drape one of the folded cloth strips over their middle finger, letting it hang down evenly on each side. Loosely holding the draped cloth, they make a fist.

Next have them go through a normal wind up delivery, with the delivery ending up with the cloth slapping their partners glove. You or your coach needs to check their delivery for proper motion, balance, and "defensive position" at the end of the follow through. Have each player do this slapping delivery 2 times, then rotate players. I would go through your group of players 2 or 3 times, then move on to another drill. Don't do this drill long, but do it often.

In the Box Control, Drill (NO.114)

This is a drill to help your pitchers develop a consistent pitching motion, get used to pitching to a player in the batter's box, and get a better feel for the strike zone. This is another drill to help pitchers develop their mechanics so that it becomes muscle memory. Run this drill out on the baseball field if at all possible. This drill can be run over in the grass, but when you run it off of the mound they become more used to the throwing off of the mound.

You will only need your pitchers, your catchers, and a stand in batter for this drill. In fact you can get more training done if you have your other pitchers and catchers working

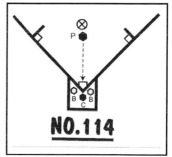

NO.114

at the same time nearby on another drill, then blow a whistle and rotate the groups. The idea is have as few kids standing around as possible.

The catcher gets down behind the plate, the batter stands in the box from the right side with a batter's helmet on. They don't swing at pitches though. After every 4 or 5 pitches have the batter alternate from the right side to the left side. The catcher calls balls and strikes on each pitch. Have your pitching coach stand out behind the pitcher and tell them what to throw. Run this drill long enough so that each of your pitchers get to make at least 15 or 20 pitches.

Only 5 or 10 pitches is not enough for them to get the feel of having a batter standing in the box. With the real little kids I would pick out who your pitchers and catchers are going to be, and not let every kid on the team do this drill because it just does not work and it's not practical. Some little kids just can't pitch a ball or get behind the plate when they are starting out.

Running Laps, Drill (NO.115)

This is a drill to help your pitchers develop stronger legs and build up their endurance. Have the real little kids run at least 1 lap around your baseball field. The bigger kids can run 2 laps. Encourage the little kids to run all the way around and not walk part of the time. Do this at every practice session right at the start of your training. Then you can set them down to rest and get a drink while you have any little talks you need with them, or tell them what they will be working on that day. They tend to be a lot more still and listen better when they are a little tired.

Sit and Hit The Target, Drill (NO.116)

This is a drill to help your pitchers throwing accuracy. They will have to throw with their elbow above their shoulder, and a good rotation of their shoulders just to get the ball to their partner How this works is two pitchers sit with their legs crossed facing each other about 20 or 30 feet between them. They have just one ball. The receiving player holds their glove in front of their face as a target. The thrower has to hit the target glove without the ball bouncing, and with a minium amount of rocking motion.

You can pair off the pitchers in rows so that no one is just standing around. I would have your pitching coach walk around and watch each pair to see how they are doing, and making sure they are doing

NO.116

it right. I would run this drill only about 20 minutes, then move on to another drill. Again the idea is always keep them busy working if at all possible. If you don't have enough coaches, then have one of your respected leader players get the group together, and run the drill.

Over the Chair, Drill (NO.117)

This is a drill to help your pitchers who like to swing their front leg way out away from their body and eventually open up or close too soon. I would say this drill is probably best for kids 12 years old and older. You should run this drill out on a baseball field where there is a mound. Get a folding chair and place the back of it on the third base side (right handers) of the pitching rubber, and close to the edge of the rubber. Place it on the first base side for left handers.

NO.117

Then have your pitchers get on the pitching rubber, assume a wind up position, and start a delivery to the plate. As their left leg rises (right handers) watch it carefully as it goes through the pitching motion and down. If their leg hits the chair at any time, then one of two things is happening.

1) They are driving the leg towards the third base side of the mound for right handers (first base side for left handers). This causes them to throw across their body.

2) They are swinging the leg open, causing their hips to open up too soon.

Then finally as the plant leg comes down, the arm comes through to the front and the back side is released. To make sure they have a good back side, the right leg must be lifted high enough so that it clears the top of the chair. This is to make sure that they are equaling out the force from their throwing arm. The experts say this will keep your pitchers from having some serious injuries. I would have each of your pitchers do this 3 times, then rotate pitchers. You will also need a catcher at the plate giving a target and catching the ball. You or your pitching coach needs to watch this drill and make corrections on the spot if necessary.

Out in Front Release Point, Drill (NO.118)

This is a drill to help your pitchers reinforce a proper release point. After they went through their short toss warm up is when you need to run this drill. What happens is when they start to do the long toss drill, and they get farther apart, their release point moves back closer to their head in an effort to get the ball up in the air to reach their partner. Some coaches say that the maximum distance that

NO.118

your pitchers should be away from each other is just far enough for their size and age to be able to reach a squatting partner while traveling through the air on a flat line. It will take some trial and error adjusting to get just the right distance for each age group.

Make sure though that they keep moving far enough apart on their long toss to throw hard on a straight line to reach their partner. It's not how far apart they can get, but that is far enough that their release point is way out in front and not back closer to their head. You or your pitching coach needs to supervise this drill to make sure they are doing it right. The drill should end up with them throwing to a squatting partner, hard and in a straight line.

If you can get your pitchers paired off in two's, and all in a row throwing at the same time, you can run this drill for only 20 minutes and accomplish a lot. Then move on to another drill.

On the Line Throwing, Drill (NO.119)

This drill is almost like Drill No.105, except it is tailored for pitchers. There is two phases to this drill though. One for throwing back and forth down on one knee, and one for winding up and throwing to a catcher at the plate. Start out by throwing in pairs

down on one knee. For the first part have two players get across from each other about 10 yards apart. Each one gets down on one knee. The push leg knee is down and the front or plant leg is up.

The pitching arm is extended straight up and out from their body, and in it's natural throwing angle to their body (over the top, 3/4, or whatever), and over their head. Then they take the hand and ball back about 6 inches and

NO.119

throw it to the partner. As they throw have them exaggerate their follow through so that they finish the motion with their arm down and outside of their front knee.

Tell your pitchers that their arm needs to be straight or almost straight when the arm is even with their body. If the elbow is bent at that point, they can not get it fully extended before they release it. A straighter arm provides a longer arc for the ball, and it will generate more velocity with less effort than when it is bent. Do this part of the drill for about 10 throws from each pitcher. Then immediately go out to the mound for the second part, while the arm motion is still fresh in their mind.

This part of the drill needs to take place where there is dirt out in front of each player. If you don't have a mound then place a pitching rubber or a simulated one in front of each player. You need to draw 3 lines out from the pitching rubber, extending towards home plate. These lines are perpendicular to the pitching rubber and should extend out. One from each corner of the rubber, and one from the center. Next your player gets up on the mound, executes their wind up and throws to home plate.

The object of this move to the plate is to come down stepping on one of the lines, depending on where they start, and keep their hips and shoulders closed during their wind up. Use this part of the drill to check and make sure they keep their hips and shoulders from opening too early, and taking velocity and accuracy away from the pitch. Have them each make 10 throws in this part of the drill, then move on to another drill.

Softball Pitching Drills

These are basically core training drills to help them improve on their pitching abilities. Make sure their arms are warmed up properly before engaging in any of these drills. They could do jumping jacks for a few minutes, or partner long toss back and forth for about 10 minutes at about 10 to 20 yards apart to accomplish this.

Pitching From the "K", Drill (NO.120)

This drill helps your pitcher in several ways. First it adds some power to their release, and secondly it squares their body to the target which makes it easier to be more consistent with their delivery. It's called the "K" because this is kind of what their body looks like when they start the drill as you would see them from the third base side.

They start the drill in the "K" position. This is where they step out in a stride, their glove hand is pointed towards the target, and their ball hand is at it's highest point. Then as they bring their ball hand around towards the release point, they push off the pitching rubber very hard (violently) with their back trailing foot so that it squares their body to the target.

NO.120

86

I would have each pitcher do this at least 10 of these at every practice session, then move on to another drill.

Running Laps, Drill (NO.121)

This drill is the same as Drill No.115. This builds up their stamina to throw harder and for longer.

Long Toss, Drill (NO.122)

This drill builds up their arm strength (speed) and accuracy. Have them start out at about 20 feet apart. Next have them pitch 10 balls to their partner. If their partner is another pitcher (best) they can pitch it back. And you can gain time to do other drills. If not, the partner just throws it back. Next have them move back in 10 yard increments until they are throwing from 60 feet if possible.

NO.122

Flat Line Work

For beginning kids you may have to adjust these distances in because they may not be strong enough yet to pitch out this far. The experts say that the maximum distance 2 pitchers should be playing long toss, is the length at which the players can pitch the ball on a relatively flat line. This they claim keeps the pitchers release point out in front of their body and avoids putting extra stress on the shoulder which is present when they release the ball at an upward angle.

Once they have maxed out their "comfortable accurate distance" for this drill, have them move to the pitching rubber at a regular softball field, and make about 20 to 30 hard pitches to a squatting catcher or partner. Some coaches found that combining the short and long distances worked on two things at the same time, their arm strength, and their accuracy. It also reestablishes a solid release point, out in front of their body and with a downward plane. Also here is another purpose it serves. It is a good drill to work on for maintaining their feel and spotting their pitches.

U.C.L.A. (a very good team) takes turns throwing 4-6 pitches each. They do this drill more at the beginning of practice. They start with fast balls, then change ups, then curve balls. They work on hitting spots, inside and outside, and executing a proper release point so that they get a good downward plane to the pitch. Do not overthrow in this drill with the little beginning kids, maybe just 2 or 3 pitches each. What you don't want to do is have them all tired out for the regular practice later on in the session.

On Their Own Wall Workout, Drill (NO.123)

Many times your pitchers want to work on their own at home on their pitching. But they can't find a catcher to come over and help. So here is what you tell them to do. Have them find a solid

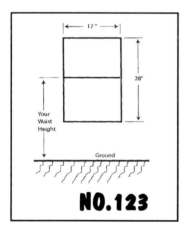

concrete or foundation brick wall, or even better is a handball court wall. Tell them to get a piece of chalk and draw a strike zone box on the wall, and make the height to their size. Next they draw a line through the middle of the box from left to right, at the same height as the belt on their waist.

Next they need to know the distance from the pitchers rubber to home plate at their level of play. If they don't know, tell them, especially the real little kids. Then they take the chalk and mark that distance, minus 2 feet, out in front of the strike zone box they have just drawn on the wall. The minus 2 feet is to compensate for where the ball would be hit by the batter. They pitch from that mark.

Tell them they need to work on their accuracy first. They should be able to catch the returning ball because if they hit the box the ball should come directly back to them. Once they get their

88

accuracy down, they can work on their speed by pitching harder. To give up their accuracy for speed is a BAD trade-off. Accuracy first, then speed is their goal.

Tell them they won't need a pitching coach or an expensive radar gun to tell them if they are throwing harder each week than they were the week before. The harder they throw, the closer the ball will return to them without hitting the ground. Tell them if they can catch the ball without it hitting the ground, or without taking a step closer to the wall, they have very good speed for their level of play. As they progress, they will notice as they catch the ball that it will have more force behind it so that they will be able to tell when they are pitching harder and faster.

Power Training

These drills are core training drills for muscle memory. They can be performed with a partner or against a wall. Also these drills should be performed with maximum speed, not slow.

The Hammer Throw, Drill (NO.124)

This may be a good drill for little kids to build up their power and speed when pitching. They will need a medicine ball for this drill. The size will depend on the size of the pitcher. How it works is they stand with their back to the target (the wall or partner). Next they bend forward, twist to one side to touch the ball to the floor, just to the outside of their foot. Their knees should be bent.

Then very hard and explosively, they swing the ball off the floor and over the opposite shoulder. They do this 2 or 3 times

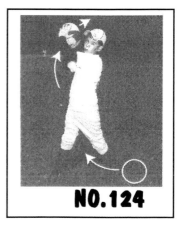

NO.124

which is a *SET*. Then switch and do a set over the other shoulder. Make sure they do this throw as hard as they can. Their partner or the wall should be far enough away that the ball reaches them. As they get stronger they can increase the distance.

The Over the Head Throw, Drill (NO.125)

This may be a good drill for little kids to build up their power and speed when pitching. They will need a medicine ball for

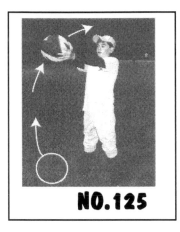

NO.125

this drill. The size will depend on the size of the pitcher. How it works is they stand with their back to the target (the wall or partner). Next they bend forward, and touch the ball to the floor between their feet. Their knees should be bent.

Then very hard and explosively, they swing the ball off the floor and over their head to the target. They do this 2 or 3 times which is a *SET*. Make sure they do this throw as hard as they can. Their partner or the wall should be far enough away that the ball just reaches them. As they get stronger they can increase the distance.

The Weighted Ball Wrist Snap Throw, Drill (NO.126)

This may be a good drill for little kids to build up their hand and ball delivery snap strength. They will need a weighted ball for this drill. They will have to make the weighted ball. Take a regular *OLD* softball and drive "6d" finishing nails into every other stitch of the ball, along the entire length of it's lace. It will take about 60 nails

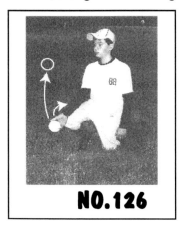

NO.126

to go around the entire length of a lace. Countersink the nails for safety. If they have a younger brother or sister, they can save the ball for them to use if they get into Softball. It's a great tool.

Have them get down on one knee (right for right handers), then take the ball in their pitching hand. Use a fast ball grip, and rest their forearm on their thigh, palm up. Next they extend their wrist and hand out over their knee.

Now they cock and snap their wrist to throw the ball straight up as far as possible. This has to be done strictly with a wrist snap. Forearm stays on the knee. I would suggest they do about 10 of these each day. If the real little kids can't do 10 then have them do 5. As the weeks go by they should notice the ball is going up higher and higher.

The Striped Ball for Pitching, Drill (NO.127)

This is a drill for teaching them the "roll peel drop" and the "rise ball". How it works is get an *OLD* softball, and paint or tape a stripe right down the middle of the ball splitting the laces, and all the way around. The reason for doing this is to visually see if the proper rotation has been imparted to the ball. The stripe gives an instant feedback to the pitcher, and is easy to see what type of rotation goes with the pitch they called. This way they won't get crossed up, and drop or miss the ball because they thought the ball was going to react differently. It's a great tool.

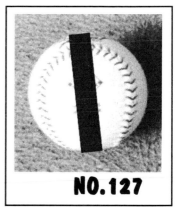

NO.127

When throwing a 'peel drop" (straight drop ball) or a "rise ball", both the pitcher and the catcher should see a solid line as the ball flies through the air towards the plate. If they do the rotation is probably correct. If the line appears to waver or they can't see it at all then the rotation is incorrect, and more practice is needed. The "straight drop" (peel drop) is released off the middle finger, palm up, as it is laid right on the stripe. The rotation would be clockwise as viewed from third base, or from top to bottom as it comes up to the plate. The wrist snap is like an uppercut punch to their chin. If any other rotation is put on the ball, the ball will not drop.

The rise ball must have counterclockwise rotation as viewed from third base, or from bottom to top as it comes up to the plate. It is released off the middle 3 fingers, palm down, with the middle finger of the 3 fingers laid right on the stripe. The wrist snap is like they suddenly reached back to scratch a fly bite behind their ear with that middle finger.

The Off Speed Pitch, Drill (NO.128)

This is a drill for teaching them the off speed pitch. Tell them that if they throw all their pitches at the same speed, a smart batter will just time their motion as to when to start their swing. The result is usually a solid hard hit ball. Explain to them that if they want to be successful, they have to take that advantage away from the batter. They need to learn how to throw all of their different pitches at different speeds, from one pitch to the next.

One coach says the best way to train a pitcher to throw just one pitch at different speeds will require a concrete wall, a tape measure, and a piece of chalk. First find a solid wall *(SEE DRILL No.123)*. Do not use a "stucco" wall, it is not very thick and will be damaged. Have them draw the strike zone box on the wall, just like in No.123. For this drill they should only be throwing to the top half of the box.

Now have them throw at the box at full speed. They keep throwing and backing up to where the ball just comes off the wall back to them without hitting the ground. Mark the point where they started that pitch with a line on the ground. That point or line is where the *100 Percent mark* is established. Next measure the distance from the wall that is the regulation throwing distance for their level of play, then subtract 2 feet. Draw another line at that point. You want this distance to be from the pitching rubber to where the batter would normally hit the ball, which is usually about 2 feet in front of the tip of home plate.

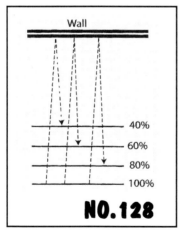

Now have the pitcher throw their slowest change up several times, then draw a line at an average distance where the ball comes back and hits the ground. Now that line has established the *40 Percent Mark*. This percentage is not perfectly accurate, but is close enough for this drill. Next measure the distance between the 100 percent mark and the 40 percent mark. Now divide that distance into 3 equal parts and draw a line at the 60 percent and 80 percent distances.

Now have your pitcher go to the 100 percent mark and pitch from there. Have them throw their fast ball, the pitch they throw with their fast ball grip. But have them put the brakes on at the end of the wind up (slows down) so that the ball only returns as far as the 60 percent mark. Now have them practice that pitch until they can consistently throw that pitch to where the ball lands nearly every time on the 60 percent line. It is very important here that they keep the wind up at 100 percent full speed, then only gently slowing it down at the last minute.

Once they are consistent at 60 percent, have them go through the same procedure at 80 percent. Then have them practice at that speed until they can consistently have the ball come back to around the 80 percent line. After they have mastered the 80 percent distance, then have them throw to the different lines on your command. Mix it up. Once they can come pretty close on all the speed lines, they are ready to try it on batters. The whole point of the drill is to get them to randomly change speeds on all their pitches, and at any time. The older kids can go through the same procedure for their curve ball or any other pitch they throw. It gives them 3 off speed pitches.

Here is a variation for the real little kids. Establish the 40 percent and 100 percent distances. Then divide the distance between them into 2 equal parts an draw a line. This is a 70 percent line. They can work on this and it will give them 2 off speeds for any of their pitches. The 100 percent distance will be accurate, the others are just estimated distances.

Hitting Drills

In this section you will find some pretty basic fundamental drills that will help your hitters, especially the little beginner kids. They should also help most of your hitters, especially if you watch them and determine they appear to not have a clue. The "T" ball drill should really help beginners.

"T" Ball Hitting Drill (NO.129)

This is a drill for teaching them to make good contact and develop muscle memory for good eye to hand coordination. When you use a batting "T" lets you practice batting techniques on a stationary ball. It allows you to make contact and develop confidence in hitting a ball. Off the "T" you can show them how to place their hits to go through the infield gaps. There are several special things to work on with beginners. Work on their hip turn, including their footwork and total body position at the point of contact. When they have that down, show them how to place their hits where they want them to go in certain situations.

Start out by showing them how to properly hold their bat. Then have them come up to the "T" take a couple of practice swings,

NO.129

without a ball, to gage their distance away from where their contact with the ball would be. For a *"basic"* stance both of their toes should be equidistant from the edge of home plate, or in the case of the batting "T" the center of the post.

The center of the barrel part of the bat should be right over the center of the "T" post. Their front foot should be approximately in line with the post. Now add the ball and let them take a couple of swings at it to get used to hitting the ball and not the post. Adjust the top of the post to the height of where the center of their strike zone would be.

As they *Start* their swing make sure they are:
1) Pivoting and turning their hips into the swing correctly.
2) Leading their swing with their front elbow.
3) Putting their hands back , and back elbow up.
4) Focusing their eyes on the ball.
5) Bending their knees.
6) Stepping with the front foot, with their toes pointing at second base.

As they *Make Contact* make sure they have:
1) Their hips squared to the front.
2) Their arms extended.
3) Their weight is centered over the back knee
4) Their eyes looking right down at the ball.

5) Their front leg straight, and the back leg bent.
6) Their chin almost right down on the shoulder of the leading arm.
7. Their wrist rolled as they make contact.

As they *Complete their Swing* make sure they:
1) Are swinging through the ball.
2) Keep their weight centered.
3) Keep their chin on their shoulder.
4) Keep their hips squared to the front.
5) Wrap their hands around their shoulder.

Once they learn all this part, then show them how to swing and contact the ball to get it to go different places. Probably the best way to do this is place the "T" out about 10 or 12 feet out in front of the field protective side screen on the field, or a tall chain link fence. Then place some kind of target on the screen that is equivalent to the height they need for hitting fly balls to the out field, line drives, or ground balls. When they can hit that target consistently, then move the "T" off center which would be about where they would have to hit ball to get it through one of the infield gaps for a single or extra base hit.

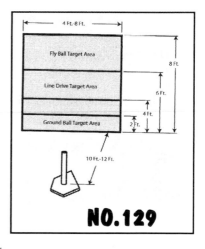

NO.129

I would take one player aside at each practice, while the rest of the team does something else, and give them 10 to 20 swings to work on this drill. Then rotate players. I would guess you could work in maybe 3 kids per practice session, depending on the time you have at night. If you have a long practice and can work in more that's even better. You just keep working them all in continuously at each practice over and over (muscle memory). Dedicate one of your coaches to do this every practice, and you should notice your hitting getting better. This technique works for hard Ball and fast pitch softball.

Here is a variation. After they have worked at hitting against a screen for several weeks, put the "T" on home plate. You will need 2 hitters for this. One hits, one sets the ball on the "T". After about 5 hits alternate hitter and setter. You can get some infield practice on the hits also. It will allow beginner players to get a comfortable feel for being at the plate. Move the "T" around on the plate.

Soft Toss Hitting Drill (NO.130)

This is a drill for teaching them to make good contact and develop muscle memory for good eye to hand coordination on a moving ball instead of the "T". This is almost like the hitting off the "T" practice, except with a team mate tossing a ball about to the same spot as when they hit off the "T". The team mate squats down off to the side of the batter and lobs the ball over so that it falls about where the batting "T" post would be. The batter then hits the ball into the screen. This makes them judge their swing so the bat head arrives at the contact point at the same time as the ball.

NO.130

I like this live hitting drill better than the "stand them at the plate and pitch to them" drill for beginners. Too many pitches are way out of the strike zone and not hittable when you use this method. In fact compared to "soft toss" it wastes time, and ties up 3 people instead of 2. You get less accomplished in the short time you have. Let each player have 10 swings then switch places with the tosser and the batter. Have them rest twice as long as they hit.

Stations

Here is another thought. You could probably set up maybe 2 or 3 soft toss stations or groups along each side on your field backstop screen fence. Or you could have one station of "T" ball hitting, then rotate to a "soft toss" station right next to it. This technique works pretty well for hard Ball and fast pitch softball.

Fine Tuning Their Concentration

The coach takes 2 balls in one hand with two fingers separating the two balls. You hold the balls as if they were stacked upon each other. Then before you toss the two balls, yell out "TOP" or "BOTTOM". This forced the hitter to actually think about which ball to hit. This fine tunes their concentration.

Pitching Behind the Hitter Drill (NO.131)

This is a drill for teaching them to NOT step back towards third base on pitches (Bailing Out). Usually these players start to "bail" before they even know where the pitch will be. Try having the batting practice pitcher throw WAY behind them on purpose every once in awhile. This is not infallible but sometimes it works. Keep telling them, "You have the bat, use it to protect yourself by hitting the ball with it".

They will see pitches all over the place, some behind them, in softball and especially in youth baseball. So here is what you do. Have them stand in the batters box and take short practice steps with the front foot towards the pitcher, over and over again. If they are really timid, tell them to step towards the second baseman (right handers). For left handers tell them to step towards the shortstop. Because they are scared of getting hit, they will probably step back towards the middle, which is where you wanted them to step anyway. After 15 or 20 steps then resume regular pitching to them.

Also sometimes you need a batter to just stand in without swinging, in a pitcher to catcher drill. Use them. They don't have to swing so have them concentrate on watching the pitch closely all the way in. This way they can practice just staying in the box, without any pressure on them to hit the ball.

NO.132

The One Handed Bunting Drill (NO.132)

This is a drill for teaching them to handle the bat for bunting. In this drill they grip the bat with their top hand right at the balance point of the bat. Then they bunt the ball holding the bat with just their one hand. All the techniques you teach such as the grip, catch the ball with the bat, and bat angle, all happen naturally with just their one hand.

The rest of the technique of adding the bottom hand to steer the ball is the easy part. You can put your players in groups of 3 or 4 for this drill. Work on this at first without a ball, then have one of the players soft toss the ball to each player with a bat. This may be too hard for at least some of the real little kids to work on because their hands are so small. However, the younger they are when you start to work with them on this drill, the better bunters they will be later on. I would let each player in the group get 6 bunts then move on to another drill.

Live Bunting With a Pitcher, Drill (NO.133)

This is a drill for teaching them to handle the bat for bunting, and get the ball to go to where they want it to go. Here is how it works. Some kind of protective screen is placed in the middle of the pitching area. This drill uses 2 pitchers and 2 catchers. The first pitcher is in front of the screen, and they throw to a batter and catcher at home plate. The second pitcher is behind the screen and throws to a batter and catcher at second base. It's probably a good idea to have 2 buckets with handles for this drill. Each pitcher takes a bucket of balls with them. Each catcher takes an empty bucket with them

The batters are divided into 2 groups, one at home plate and one at second base. All the balls that the batter misses are put into the catchers bucket. This lets the pitcher get ready quicker for the next batter. You or your coach tells the batters which type of bunt to make, bunt for a hit, sacrifice bunt, or drag bunt. If they make contact the batter at home runs to first, then goes to the end of the other line. If the batter at second makes contact they run to third base , then go to the end of the other line. Every

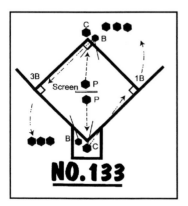

NO.133

bunter should get a chance to make contact 3 times, then rotate to the next player. When all players have had their chance then move on to another drill.

Bat Speed, Drill (NO.134)

This is a drill for teaching them to increase their bat speed. There are 3 different routines one coach uses to help kids with a slow bat speed (beginners that swing after the ball is in the catchers mitt). He does this using the "soft toss" technique. The routines run like this:

1) Have them put a weighted donut on their everyday bat. Then hit 5 baseballs or softballs with it.
2) Have them get a long thin fungo bat and hit 5 balls.
3) Then last have them hit 5 balls with their everyday bat.

This same coach says, "Do 2 sets of this drill 2 or 3 times a week.". Then after 4 to 6 weeks you should see a positive increase in their bat speed.

Hands to the Ball, Drill (NO.135)

This is a drill for teaching them to get their hands around and on the ball. Using this drill helps them to move their head and eyes to the ball. This is a pretty effective *"Softball"* core training drill (muscle memory). Softball requires quick reaction because the ball gets to you very quick with the pitcher so close. Here is how it works. Have the batter stand about 3 feet from the backstop screen or

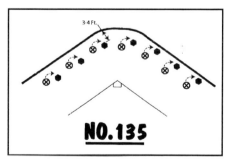

fence. They get in their regular batting stance, and face the fence or screen. With one exception though, they have their bat resting on their shoulder.

You, one of your coaches, or even another player, soft toss the ball up to them. The batter has to hit the ball with only the butt (end cap on the handle) of the bat. NO SWINGING is allowed, they just have to quickly put the bat end cap on the ball. The ball can be tossed up either high, low, inside, or outside. Another way to explain it to them is put their nose to the ball, and the eyes will follow. You could split this drill up into pairs all the way around the backstop screen and get more training accomplished in a short time.

Eye on the Ball, Drill (NO.136)

Here are several drills for teaching them to see the ball better. If you have young players that seem to have good hitting mechanics, but they are not hitting the ball, these drills should help them see the ball better. These are all pretty effective *"Softball"* drills. But they can work for most little kids in hard ball also.

Balls and Strikes

Have the player in question stand in the batters box, and just watch the ball come in to the catcher. NO SWINGS, all they have to do is CALL "balls" and "strikes" on each pitch. The best thing for learning to watch the ball is just seeing lots of live pitching. They learn to read the different pitches, and the pitcher gets better practice when there is a batter in the box.

The Miss, Miss, and Hit Technique

You use a series of 3 pitches for them to learn how to see the ball. On the first pitch they have to swing over the top of the ball. On the second pitch they swing under the ball. On the third pitch they have to hit the ball dead center if possible. Keep repeating this drill until they can do it right every time. Give the batter at least 5 tries. Then take it up with them at next practice if necessary. Also with the little kids you might want to bring the pitcher in closer, where the pitches have a better chance of being in the strike zone.

Hitting Different Objects

Use anything for them to try and hit, white whiffle balls, plastic snap on lids (thrown like frisbees), or anything that is smaller then the usual baseball or softball. And something that does not necessarily move in a straight line. They will have to concentrate on the object just to see it.

Two-Ball Soft Toss

You need two different color baseball whiffle balls for this technique. One could be white and one red. Or you could mark half of the balls with a different color dot. Also you could use golf whiffle balls. And it's probably going to be easier to toss the smaller balls.

Plus the batter will have to use more coordination and really focus to be able to hit just one of the two smaller balls. Either one, not both. The pitcher tosses 2 balls up at the same time, and with just one hand. At first the batter just has to hit one ball. Then to make it harder, tell them which ball you want them to hit, RED or WHITE. The pitcher may have to be up closer for this technique also. Give each batter 6 tries to hit just one ball, and 6 tries for the called color.

Soccer Ball Hitting, Drill (NO.137)

Here is a *Softball* drill used by the University of Mississippi. They use this to: 1) Build forearm strength. 2) Teach players how to see the rotation on the ball. When they hit it they want back spin. 3) Teach young beginning hitters to drive through the ball when they hit it. Here is how it works.

You will need a batting "T", a small bathroom plunger, 3 or 4 soccer balls, and an old bat. You put the plunger upside down into the top of the "T". Then put the soccer ball on top of the plunger. Have your players line up like a regular "T" ball hitting drill against a screen, except hit the soccer ball and try for back spin.

Have one of the waiting players put the soccer ball in place. Let each player have 10 hits and switch. You can run this drill on the side while another drill is going on, then rotate players in pairs.

On One Knee Hitting, Drill (NO.138)

Here is a *Softball* drill to let your batters concentrate on the proper hand and arm movement without worrying about their legs. Here is how it works. Set up a net or pitch back with a mat in front of it. Place a medium size orange cone on the mat. Your batters kneel down on their back knee. Their front leg should be up and straight out in front towards the net. Place a ball on top of the cone, and have them hit it into the net.

NO.138

You can have pairs, one player hits and the other feeds balls on the cone. Have them make 10 hits then switch places. You can run this drill on the side while another drill is going on, then rotate players to another group in pairs.

Catcher Drills

In this section you will find some pretty basic fundamental drills that will help your catchers, especially the little beginner kids. They should learn concentration, agility, and quick reactions. Catchers need to be smart, they are like a quarterback on the field most of the time. If your catcher is not a leader, and does not listen to instructions, you will have a problem teaching them much of any thing. And because of that your team will have some problems. You may want to step back and see who you have picked as your catchers. I would have at least two, and maybe one or two other kids who can fill in there if they are needed for a game.

Learn Not to Flinch, Drill (NO.139)

Here is a drill to help your catchers learn to trust their equipment. They have to learn to keep their eyes on the ball when

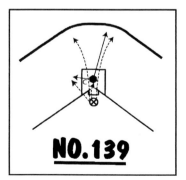

NO.139

it comes off the bat, or when it skips off the dirt. If they flinch and pull their head back, it exposes their throat. This is a problem with young beginning catchers.

Have your catcher squat down and get into their ready position, then a coach or one of your players stands out about 2 or 3 feet in front of them. They get a ball in each

102

hand, then with a quick flick of the thrower wrist, they throw one ball directly at the catchers mask. At the same time they lob the other ball up in the air with the other hand. The catcher has to locate the pop up, come up, and catch it with two hands. The ball can be lobbed away from the catcher so they can work on diving catches. And it can also be lobbed over their head and close to the fence or backstop so they can work on foul balls in that area

The object of flicking the ball at the mask is to get them used to balls hitting their mask. I would have them catch or go after 5 pop ups in front, 5 balls they have to dive out or to the side for, and 5 foul balls back near the fence or backstop. The rotate to the next catcher. You can hardly ever train enough catchers because some times they don't make the game or they get hurt.

Glove to the Ball- Knees to the Glove Drill (NO.140)

Here is a drill to help your catchers learn to block balls away from them, direct them towards the plate, and throw down to bases effectively. Theses are two of the hardest basic skills to teach catchers. They take the longest to develop. So if that's the case with your catchers, then you may want to try and find a catcher coach and designate them to work with your catchers as much as possible. The rule to remember is "Glove to the Ball - Knees to the Glove".

One of the big difficulties is many catchers try to do it just the opposite way. Here is how this works. Start out with your catcher squatting down in their ready position, and without their glove. Then 3 balls are arranged in a shallow triangle, in front of them, but behind the plate. The first ball is

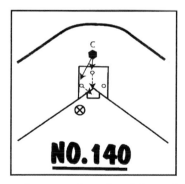

arranged dead center behind the plate, the second to the right and forward, the third to the left and forward. Number 2 and 3 balls are even with each other.

First Part-Blocked Ball to Plate

Coach yells, GO", the catcher falls forward to the center ball on their hands, then brings both knees up to their hands.

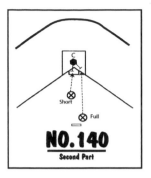

Emphasizing the angle their body has be in, they bump and deflect the ball onto the home plate. They do this with all 3 of the balls. Have them each do a set of 3 about 5 times without their full gear on. The coach or one of the other catchers puts the balls back in place each time.

Now they put their glove on and go through another set of 3 the same way for 5 times, still without full gear. Make sure they put their glove to the ball first, cup the ball, then bring their knees to the glove. Then rotate catchers until they all get a chance to work on this.

Second Part- Full Gear Blocking

Have them put on their full gear and get in their normal stance behind the plate. Then the coach goes out in front of the plate a little ways and short tosses a tennis ball, or a ball that is soft, on the ground towards the plate. Catcher blocks the ball by glove first, then knees to the ball. Do about 10 of these, then rotate catchers. If you don't have enough coaches, then the waiting catcher can act as the coach so that you can run this drill at least 2 times a week.

Third Part- Full Distance Blocking

Same process, soft balls, but coach tosses balls from the mound.

Fourth part- Hard Balls with Short Throws

Fifth Part- Full Distance Throws, Medium Speed to Called Area

Sixth Part- Full Distance Hard Throws to Called Area

Seventh Part- Full Distance Hard Throws to Varied Areas

Once you are satisfied with their development, work with them regularly for about 20 blocks and throw downs, 10 at a session. Make sure you work your catchers in pairs when possible. The final step is block the ball then get up, recover it, and throw down to a base.

Foul Ball Pop Flies Drill (NO.141)

Here is a drill to help your catchers learn to catch foul ball pop flies around the plate area. This will be hard for little beginning kids to learn, but keep working with them. Use lots of reps.

Have your catcher get down in their normal squat position behind the plate. The coach stands somewhere behind the plate area, and throws a pop fly ball up in the air. The coach yells, "FOUL". Now at this point there are several ways for the catcher to react. One, the catcher looks up and locates the foul, then throws their mask off and out of the way in a direction where they won't trip over it.

The other way is the pitcher points to the catcher, and indicates the direction of the foul. Next knowing the direction, the catcher throws off their mask the other way, and then looks up for the ball without the mask. This way they can see it better. Throw up about 6 pop foul fly balls for each of your catchers. Then move on to another drill.

Pop Up Throwing Cross Drill (NO.142)

Here is a softball drill to help your catchers learn to pop up and throw down to a base. This will be hard for the little kids to do. But if you keep working on it with them, they will learn. This is basic catcher throwing mechanics.

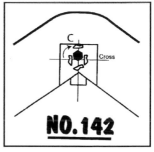

Here is how it works. To start the drill have your catcher squat down in their normal catching stance. Draw a horizontal line in the dirt right through their two feet. Now they draw another line right between their feet going vertical out towards the pitcher, and crossing the other line forming a cross.

Now without a ball you or one of your coaches yell out, "STEAL". The catcher pops up, turns in the air, and lands on the vertical line. As a good practice technique have them hold onto their ear as they pop up each time. Have them do this 6 times, then switch catchers. The coach then goes out and makes a short throw to them. They extend their glove, make the catch, bring their glove arm, with the ball, in and across their chest, take the ball out and cock their throwing arm back. And they do this all while popping up and at the same time turning 90 degrees so that their feet land on the vertical line. Make sure they catch the ball then pop up all as one quick continuous motion. Have them do this 6 times for each catcher. Also make sure they are bringing their hand with the ball up to their ear each time

Soft Hands Drill (NO.143)

Here is a softball drill to help your catchers learn to have soft hands as they catch the ball. A lot of catches in a short period

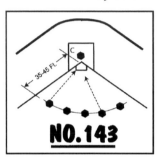

NO.143

of time will teach them to have soft hands. Have 5 players go out about 35 to 45 feet away from home plate. And within about a 65 degree arc. In turn each one throws a ball at the squatting catcher in full gear. The catcher has to quickly properly receive the ball, frame it, and drop it because e the balls are going to come rapid fire.

Just as the catcher is starting to drop the first ball, the next player should be in the motion of throwing the second ball. It goes around to the end and then back to the first player. The catcher needs to catch 25 balls rapid fire. As the catchers get better, you can increase the number of balls thrown and the pace at which they are thrown.

If you don't have 5 balls for each player to throw, you will need a shagger to step in when the players run out of balls, pick them all up from in front of the plate and take them back with a bucket starting with the first player, feeding them from behind, so the drill can resume. The idea is for the catchers to catch 25 balls in a short period of time. You rotate catchers after 25 balls. Then move on to another drill.

Soft Quick Hands Drill (NO.144)

Here is a softball drill to help your catchers learn to have soft and quick hands. The catchers stand across from each other without a glove. Their feet are shoulder width apart. Their hands are shoulder width apart at stomach height. Then they take a ball in one hand and toss it from hand to hand up in air using about a 2 or 3 feet arc. They do this for about 30 seconds.

Then gradually they decrease the height of the arc and speed up the hand transfers. They keep doing this until the ball is flying back and forth between hands almost in a straight line. Have them do this for about 5 to 10 minutes, then move on to another drill. This is similar to juggling, except with just one ball and faster.

Side to Side Speed Drill (NO.145)

Here is a softball drill you can use to help your catchers learn to move from side to side, and be able to get their body in front of the ball so that it never gets away from them. It also helps increase your speed. Here is how it works. Have your coach or the other catcher stand out about half way to the mound in front of the plate.

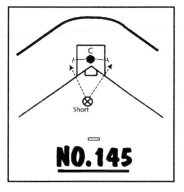

Then the coach gets a bucket of balls, and starts to throw or pitch balls to both sides of the catcher. Not too far away, but maybe about 3 or 4 feet away from the catcher.

Start out at shorter distances away then gradually increase the distance as they get better. The catcher gets into full gear down in their normal position. As soon as they see the ball is going to their side, they jump out to the side, stop or block the ball, then they push it out in front of them and go back to the plate for the next throw. This is very tiring, but it builds their strength up. I would make about 10 throws, then let them take a short rest. Try to make at least 20 throws, then rotate the catchers.

Stealing Throw Down Drill (NO.146)

Here is a softball or hard ball drill you can use to help your catchers learn to throw down to any base quickly and effectively to nail stealers, or throw out advancing runners. You, one of your coaches, or if you are short coaches, one of your leader players, stand out to one side of the mound about half way there with a bucket of balls.

Your catcher squats down in their normal position in full gear. Then the coach throws or pitches the ball to the catcher at medium speed

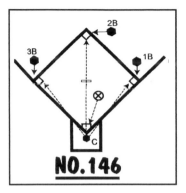

at first. Then speed up the throws as your catchers get better. The catcher takes the throw, pops up and guns a throw to *whichever base* you call out. Have them make 3 throws to each of the 3 bases, then rotate catchers. Pay particular attention to their throws to second (longest). After 2 sets for each catcher move on to another drill.

Balls Out in Front of the Plate Throw Down Drill (NO.147)

Here is a softball or hard ball drill you can use to help your catchers learn to quickly one hand field the ball, then throw down to any base quickly and effectively. Take 6 balls and spread them out in an area in front of the plate. The coach or a player stands off to the side to direct the throws. Your catcher squats down in their normal position in full gear. Then at your call of, "GO" - then "THE BASE", they pop up, run out and pick up any of the balls with one hand, and gun a throw down to whichever base you have called out. Have them make 2 throws to each base, then rotate catchers. Pay particular attention to their throws to second (longest). After 2 sets for each catcher, move to another drill.

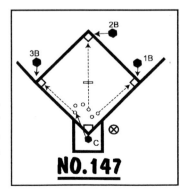